Skipping Between The Raindrops

A MEMOIR

By *JA Rinker*

Copyright

© Copyright 2020 JARinker.
All rights reserved.

No part of this book may be reproduced, stored in a retrieval system, or transmitted by any means, electronic, mechanical, photocopying, recording, or otherwise, without written permission from both the author and publisher of this book. .

ISBN-13:   978-1-941345-79-5   Paperback
ISBN-E: 978-1-005259-55-6
ASIN: B08MMZTB6N   Kindle

Printed in the United States
Designed by Kathleen J. Shields

Canyon Lake, TX
www.ErinGoBraghPublishing.com

Acknowledgements

Dedication

Skipping Between The Raindrops is dedicated to my family and to my many friends who have helped me *skip between the raindrops* a multitude of times.

Blessings

I could not have finalized this book without the able assistance of my copy editor, Dara Zoboroski. She has made a miraculous effort of ascertaining what I dictated into the iPad. In addition, her computer skills at finding synonyms, word-phrasing, and fact finding have been a welcome contribution to *Skipping Between The Raindrops*.

Many thanks go to Melba Robbins, proofreader – par excellence. She deserves many thanks for adding zillions of commas, semicolons, quotation marks, etc., etc., and so forth. In addition, she was instrumental for turning the word "things" into a million *different* words.

And to both Dara and Melba for spending a week with me reading and rereading the final draft in order to catch any mistakes – KUDOS and BLESSINGS!

My fervent thanks go to Kathy Hoy-Gipe for proofing the proofers. There can never be too many bubbles in the champagne.

And finally, my heartfelt thanks to my publisher Kathleen J. Shields, founder of Erin Go Bragh Publishing Company, for all her advice and creative genius on the book cover and page formatting. Her suggestions were very much appreciated.

Table of Contents

Prologue - Let Me Introduce Myself 1
Part I - From Whence I Came Down On The Farm 4
    The Bonds Of Family 5
    The Homestead 12
    The Down And Dirty Work In The Fields...........................26
    The Miscellaneous Memories Of Childhood........................31
    Brotherly Love - My Hero And My Cohort In Crime 40
    The Games We Played Down On The Farm 45
    The Games We Played In Town 48
    The Game Of Life – Bridge 49
    Hooked On Smokin' 52
    The Social Graces And Gatherings Of The Time.................56
    The Radio Waves Saved The Days And Nights....................61
    In Good Times And Bad Fostering The Ties That Bind 63
    The Etiquette Of Making Social Calls 66
    Summer Fun - Concerts, Movies & Hixson's Pond 73
Part II - My Grade School Debut 79
    Learning The Ropes..80
    Rules To Live By 88
    Grades 2, 3, And Wonderful 4..90
    Final Year Of Grade School 94
    Meandering Home 97
    School Happenings 99
    Playtime 101
    The Most Popular Game in School – Marbles....................105

The End Of Grade School 108
Part III - My Junior High School Promotion........................ 109
Onward And Upward 110
Skipping The 7th Grade 117
New Friends 119
My 8th Grade Shenanigans 125
Holiday Festivities Through The Years 131
Part IV - Grand Finale - My High School Years 138
My Exciting Summers 139
The Party Line 143
Summer Music Camp 145
Church Activities 146
I Cross The Divide - Trego Community High School 149
Good Teachers 150
Physical Education? 155
Varsity Sports 157
Intramural Activities 160
My Best Friend 161
A No Show 165
Crazy Escapades 167
A Beautiful Winter's Day 169
Odds and Ends 171
How Can This Be? 175
The Smoking Saga Continues 177
Throw In A Little Beer Miller?   High Life? 180
Making Music 182
My Sis, Dianne 185

Remember "Jathon, Call Me Thandy Ott"? 188
Back To Tennis 190
Our Exciting Senior Sneak 191
The End Of High School 193
Onto The Next Life Adventures 194
Epilogue 195
Catastrophic Events 195
Bonus Sections 199
Quirky Dictation Bloopers - My Tribute To Technology! ... 200
Old-Timey Jokes And Cheers 217
Autographs From My Classmates 222
Recipes From The Homestead 231
Order Forms 243
Be On The Lookout 245
Why Not Share Your Story? 246
Author Biography 247

Prologue

Let Me Introduce Myself

Hi there! Let me introduce myself. My name is Judy Rinker (alias JARinker).

Through the years it has been my practice to keep a journal with the dream of someday writing a book. In 1974, I sat down and began to organize my notes. This proved to be a very short term project as life got in the way. Thirty-two years later in 2006, after retiring from operating Harambe Oaks guest ranch in Fischer, Texas, I finally typed my notes into a computer and printed what I had compiled up to that time.

Then I became involved in Fischer and Canyon Lake community activities, and the memoir project got buried once again. Due to the Covid-19 Pandemic of 2020, I have been "compelled" to "stay at home". This meant no bridge playing, no eating out, no shopping, no visiting, and no parties to organize or to host on the patio and deck. Rather than sitting around crying about the injustice of the pandemic, I have unearthed my memoir notes, and 46 years later I am finally achieving my dream of writing and publishing my youthful anecdotes. This has all been accomplished by G.O.I.P.! (Growing Old In Place!)

Why the title *Skipping Between The Raindrops*? From my Western Kansas roots, I believe I have led a Cinderella life. Who would've thunk it? Along the way, I developed a passion for traveling, although our family almost never took a vacation. Until I was seventeen I had only been to Colorado twice and once to the Black Hills of South Dakota. As a teacher I was free during the summers, as a result, I have *skipped between the raindrops* in all fifty states, a hundred countries (more or less), all seven continents, and sailed the seven seas. I have been gainfully employed in Alaska, Iowa, Utah, California, New York, Pennsylvania, Massachusetts, Kansas, Texas and Israel.

I have skied in Utah, Massachusetts, California, and the Alps in Switzerland; I've ridden camels in Egypt; safaried in Africa; viewed the Shah's jewels in Iran; sipped tea with a champion Sumo wrestler in Japan; hot-air ballooned in Australia; viewed the Taj Mahal in India up close and personal; talked with penguins at the South Pole; preached a sermon in the Chapel at Yosemite National Park; led singing on a cruise ship bound for Alaska; floated down the Rhine River in Germany; hiked the wild trails in Ireland and canoed the clear lakes of the Quetico in Canada. I have been to seven Olympics on four continents and traveled around the world twice. Some of these adventures were solo and some were shared with friends, each contributing to my fantastic journey of *Skipping Between The Raindrops* and making new friends around the world.

My Zodiac sign is Aquarius and the description suits me to a T. Ruled by the planet Uranus, Aquarians are unusual and different. Although likely to be misunderstood by others, they are usually ahead of others in thought and action. Uranus is electrical, magnetic, sensational and extraordinary and has an undue influence on Aquarians. They achieve what others deem impossible even though they are not always correct in judging practical matters. Their success depends upon friendships. A friend recently described me as a "People Collector". Well, yes, actually isn't that what Aquarians do - create friendships?

This book shares the tales, anecdotes and memories, as far as I can recollect, about becoming a confident young woman desiring to explore the people and places of the world. The lessons that I learned living on a Kansas wheat farm gave me the wisdom to choose among all the various opportunities presented to me and empowered me to lead a charmed life. My independent self was nurtured by a number of factors: parents who were educated and concerned about my well-being, entertainment which was to a great degree self-created, chores which had to be done (and done well) and a mind filled with curiosity. All these influences provided a firm foundation and enabled me to pursue a higher education, to risk venturing into new experiences and to accomplish most of my lifelong passions and goals.

Part I

From Whence I Came Down On The Farm

I was raised on a farm five miles east of WaKeeney, Kansas. It's a community located in Western Kansas along US-40, now Interstate 70, halfway between Denver and Kansas City. Named for its founders Albert Warren and James Keeney in 1879, it was typical of small town America in the mid-Twentieth Century.

The Bonds Of Family

The Family

My immediate family consisted of my Dad, Mother, two siblings and myself. My Dad's name was Frank Bryan Rinker and my Mother's name was Hermena Virginia Rinker. My brother Franklin Eugene (named after President Franklin D. Roosevelt) was three and one-half years older than I and my sister Dianne is six and one-half years younger than I. *Please note I'm not disclosing my age. Ha! Also please note that my brother had a middle name but neither my sister nor I were given one. I always found that an interesting little factoid.*

My brother, Gene, notably appears as a supporting character in a number of my antics. This narrative of my young life rarely mentions my sister, Dianne, as she was far enough behind me in age that our lives seldom intertwined - *sad, but true.*

My Dad Frank **My Mom Hermena**

Mom & Dad

Best Pals - Gene & Judy

The Family of Four **The Family of Five**

Me, Myself and I – Judy

My Brother Gene

My Sis Dianne

My Dad

My Dad was born on the homestead where I grew up. He graduated from high school in WaKeeney and then attended the University of Kansas in Lawrence. During his freshman year of college, he joined the army (1917-1918), served several months during World War I, but never left the United States. He then returned home to the farm.

Upon the death of his parents the land was divided equally among the siblings. Dad began to farm his share along with two of his sisters' shares and some nearby acreage which he purchased. I never thought of our family as being rich or poor; we were just doing the best we could. Dad practiced the philosophy of "never wasting any money". This viewpoint contributed to his accomplishment in becoming a successful farmer even during the Depression and the Dust Bowl days of the 1930's.

My Mom

Mother was born in Bushong in eastern Kansas with its rolling hills, picturesque rock walls and a plethora of greenery. After graduating from Emporia State Teachers College, Mother rode the train out to WaKeeney to begin a new life on the flatland prairies of Western Kansas. I imagine the stark, treeless and flat Western Kansas landscape took her by surprise. She taught English, speech and drama in Trego Community High School. During her several years of teaching, she met Dad, married and settled down to the life of a full-time farmer's wife. She never taught school again although my brother Gene, my sister Dianne and I were her star pupils for many years to come.

When my Mother was very young, her father was killed by a ricochet gunshot and her mother took in sewing to make ends meet. Upon graduation from high school, both my Mother and her sister, Edith, taught for a time in country grade schools. This enabled both of them, as well as their brother, Ira, to attend college - a unique occurrence in the early to mid-1920's.

The Relatives

Almost all of my parents' relatives lived elsewhere, so we seldom saw them. The relatives we did see were Dad's half-brother Roy, who farmed the property next to us, his half-brother Harry who lived in WaKeeney, his sister, Blanche, who lived in the area and my Mother's mother, who lived in eastern Kansas.

The Homestead

The House In The Dust Bowl Days

As a care-free, wild child romping in the fields surrounding the homestead, I vaguely remember the disastrous Dust Bowl days of the mid-1930's. At that time, our house was a wooden structure, so particles oozed in from the dust stirred up by the traffic on the unpaved road and from the dirt plowed up by Dad from the land on three sides of our house. I do remember as a baby, Mother putting a wet washcloth over my face while I was in bed so I could breathe. I have pictures of Gene and me playing on mounds of dirt three to four feet high as if they were snow banks. Later, when I was a little older, I can remember a dust storm rolling in. We were in town shopping, and in order to get across the street to our parked car, a number of people had to form a human chain.

This Old House

After the Dust Bowl years, when I was around three to five years old, we moved to town while Dad converted our wood house to brick. At first, we lived in a small rented house close enough to the grade school so that Gene could walk to school. When that house was sold, we moved into the Deines apartments, which were right downtown. I don't remember anything about the original wood house, but I loved the brick home which Dad built around the old one. Looking back, I am puzzled as to how my folks were able to afford all this right after the Depression. I never thought to ask them about it while they were alive.

The New Home with Hammock Trees

A Comfy Home, Now Treasured Memories

The folks had some beautiful antique furniture, some of which graces my present home. There's a beautiful set of 1860's cherry wood furniture: a rocking chair, a straight back chair and a loveseat. They have been refinished and reupholstered and are in fantastic shape. I have the cherry wood rocking chair in my living room and my sis has the other two pieces, as well as the baby grand piano. I have an oak rocking chair from the 1880's in my bedroom. In addition, I have the high chair which we all used, my baby buggy and my cradle, as well as book-cases, end tables, pictures and hundreds of photographs from a bygone age.

Where The Action Took Place - The Kitchen And The Dining Room

The front door of the house was used only for guests. We entered the house by walking from the garage to the enclosed side porch, and into the galley-style kitchen. One side consisted of a propane stove, double sink with drainage surfaces on each side and a garbage can next to the door leading to the enclosed porch. The opposite side had counters and over-head cabinets on either side of the door leading into the dining room. In the dining room were the Servel ice box, a buffet, a small corner cabinet, a pull-down ironing board, a built-in telephone box, a large rectangular, extendable oak table and eight padded oak chairs.

Out of this small kitchen came the most delectable foods. Mom's fried chicken was extraordinary as were her meatloaf, baked chicken, pork chops, roast beef, pork roast, salmon patties, ham steaks, Swiss steak, scalloped potatoes,

Spanish rice, and various fruit and vegetable dishes; some which graced our table every meal. Everything was always cooked to perfection - except for the mushrooms in the gravy and the asparagus (more on these later). Mother made the best breads, *pies*, cakes and cookies in the world. I really don't remember ever having a loaf of store-bought bread in the house. We had fresh, hot, made from scratch cinnamon rolls many mornings. We were all expected to be at the table every morning for a full-course breakfast – no excuses. Our school lunch sandwiches were also made with homemade bread. Supper included fresh hot rolls (Parker House rolls being my favorite). *Mother used a lot of yeast!* In the winter the big meal of the day was supper at 5:30 pm and in the summer our main meal was lunch at 12 noon.

See recipes from the Rinker kitchen at the back of the book!

My brother, an imaginative cook as well, could make the most awesome angel food cake from scratch! When Gene was a senior in high school, he managed to talk the principal into offering a cooking class for boys and most of the upper class guys signed up for it. However, I really think the popularity of the class was due to the crush they had on the teacher.

We Had To Taste Everything – Or Else

Although I liked most foods, there were several I couldn't tolerate. The asparagus episode comes to mind. One summer lunch we all sat down to our big meal of the day. Lo and behold, there appeared upon my plate a spoonful of asparagus. I had never seen it before, but I'm certain Mom thought it would be a good edible vegetable for me to learn to eat. After I took the first bite, I looked Mother straight in the eye and said, "I'm not eating that! I don't like it!" Her reply was "Yes, you're going to eat it or else you're going to get a spanking."

After sitting at the table for three hours, at 3:00 pm, I still hadn't eaten it and sure enough I got the spanking. I never ate asparagus again until I was in my 70s when my housemate grew some in the garden. I cut it into small pieces, threw it in a stir-fry and sure enough I found it edible.

Living By Dad's Tidbits Of Wisdom

Although most of my life lessons were learned by example, my Mother and Dad did have some words of wisdom occasionally – *imagine that!* A small bathroom off our kitchen was where we washed our hands before and brushed our teeth after meals. On one occasion, Dad asked me if I had brushed my tongue. Up to that time I had never given it a thought. *Now, to this day, when I brush my tongue, I think of Dad and his Words of Wisdom.*

Laundry Chores

Back in the mists of my memory the wringer washing machine was in the basement. All the clothes had to be taken downstairs to wash and then carted back upstairs, through the hallway, dining room, kitchen and porch to the clothesline in the chicken yard for drying. That presented itself to be a backbreaking chore! Later, the old-time wringer washing machine was moved to the porch. I was always afraid Mom would get her hands or arms caught in the wringer. I would take the basket of wet clothes out to the chicken yard and hang them on the clothesline. *I rather enjoyed that job.* After the wind dried the clothes, I took them off the line and brought them back to the house where Mom would then iron everything, except our underwear. We even ironed the pillowcases and sheets. Later on, we got a fabric linen press ironer (the size of a treadle sewing machine) which was great for pressing sheets, towels, pillowcases and pants – not so good for blouses and shirts. The ironer resided in the basement, so all the ironer clothes had to be carted downstairs and then back upstairs. One saving grace of the ironing chore was that the ironing board was built into the wall in the dining room. All one had to do was open the door and let it down; this was a welcome convenience.

Aside: Later in her life, Mom finally got an automatic washer and dryer installed on the porch. However, she really didn't like the dryer as she much preferred the smell of fresh-air-dried clothes from the outdoor clothesline.

More Chores - Milking

We had milk cows which Dad, Gene and I milked on our one-legged stools in the pasture. This job I was not especially fond of as I didn't even care for milk unless incorporated into ice cream or butter. We did churn our own butter ... sort of fun, but I always felt it took a long time for the butter to show up. The milk separator resided in the basement. The fresh milk had to be carried downstairs, separated, and then carried upstairs to put the milk and cream in the icebox. Then, all the parts of the separator had to be carried up the stairs to the kitchen sink, washed, dried and carried back downstairs. A diary entry in 1945 reads: *Churned butter this morning.* We churned our own butter all through World War II. *Life was not easy "back in the day".*

Never-Ending Chores

Mother was a loving mother, but she was also a stern taskmaster. If she asked you to do something, she expected it to be done, not later, but immediately. Mother and I did most of the dusting of the house and Dad usually vacuumed. Dad and I took out the trash and we burned the burnables in one cylinder and put the wet garbage in another to compost. I would also help in the garden. My tasks included hoeing weeds, snapping green beans, shelling peas, husking corn, and cleaning lettuce, radishes and carrots.

Daddy, Where Does Fried Chicken Come From?

We had chickens much of the time, so there were always chicken coops to clean, eggs to gather and the chicken yard to rake. I hated the chore part, but loved to consume fried chicken, especially my favorite piece - the neck!

However, I will never forget my first (and last) foray into the killing and cleaning of a chicken. Dad and I chased a chicken (poor thing) until we caught it and hacked its head off on the chopping block. We carried the headless chicken upside down with its neck dripping blood out to the light tower. Then Mom brought out a large tea kettle of boiling water and poured it over the chicken which had been placed in a bucket. We took it out of the bucket, sat on the rungs of the light tower and plucked off its feathers. After being a part of this slaughter, taking the chicken to the kitchen, burning off the pinfeathers over the propane flame of the stove and experiencing the awful smell of scorched pinfeathers, I have never been able to stand the thought of eating the neck again.

Dad's evening relaxation pose was to lie on the floor and read with his feet up.

The Lawn Mower And Coffee Wake-Up Calls

As Dad did the yard work early in the morning, one of his favored ways to tease me would be to mow right under my bedroom windows. He knew that the sound of the engine racket soaring upwards through the open windows would jar me awake and he was right. Another annoyance which would disturb me was the smell of coffee wafting throughout the house and upstairs to my room. The aroma of coffee made my stomach churn. I never did like that smell and I still don't. I find it strange that although both my parents drank coffee every morning and at most social occasions, none of us children grew up to drink coffee.

__Aside:__ To this day, I still have never tasted coffee, still do not like the smell nor do I like anything flavored with coffee.

The Exciting Nights On The Upstairs Porch

My brother's room was upstairs at the end of the hallway. He had a door leading out to a porch with an external stairway that went down to a short sidewalk leading to the Springhouse and the garage.

Once in a while he and I, or a friend or two staying overnight, carted our pillows and blankets onto the porch to sleep. The porch just had a tar paper covering, sloped slightly for rain runoff and was void of any safety railings. Sleep was always iffy - yet exciting for two reasons: 1) there was the fear of either rolling off onto the hard ground below or sleepwalking off (I was prone to sleepwalking when I was younger) and 2) the panoramic views of the night sky were so spectacular that we often stayed awake for hours watching the Big and Little Dippers, Orion, the Milky Way and a million other twinkling, glorious constellations. We had contests to see who could count the most falling stars.

The melodies of the night kept us awake for many an hour - the buzz of the katydids, the chirp of the crickets and the whip of the whip-poor-wills, but the distant whistle of the Union Pacific night train a mile and one-half south, headed from Kansas City to Denver, eventually lulled us into a restless sleep.

The Perplexing Garage "Opening"

The double car garage was approximately 40 feet away from the house. On the front end of the garage Dad built a concrete slab for parking and installed a pull-up double door. But the perplexing part of the garage was the side nearest to the house. The shortest way to get to the house from the garage was by climbing through an "opening" that Dad had cut out of the wall. The opening was 24" from the ground and 24" wide and approximately 4 feet high. The "opening" had a make-shift door that consisted of the cut out wall section with hinges on one side. We continually had to crawl over this inconvenient 24" hurdle, while ducking our heads to enter and to exit the garage. *To this day, I am bewildered why there was never a real door installed, but at the time, we all accepted the status quo.*

The House, Windmill, Springhouse, Hudson in Garage and Dianne

The Springhouse And Whims Of The Wind And The Sun

The Springhouse was located between our enclosed side porch and the garage. It was a 12' x 12' stone-walled building on the ground floor and a wood-framed structure on the second story enclosing a water tank. To the right of the Springhouse was the windmill. Early on, if the wind didn't blow, the only water available for use was the water stored in the tank. At some point, Dad installed a gas powered pump so having water was not determined by the whims of the wind.

There existed in the Springhouse a shoulder-high faucet from which we often drank as the water flowed ice cold, and two side-by-side showerheads in the ceiling. In the summer, we took showers in the Springhouse. The shower water drained via an underground pipe into the garden. Hot water was obtained from the sun-heated 20 or so gallon water tank attached to the south side of the second story wooden structure. Hence, the hot water usually made it through two showers, but if you were the third person you were often out of luck. After showering, we would dash to the windmill to grab our towels. Then, we would wrap our towels around us and run through the house to our various bedrooms drip-drying along the way. Oh, what fun!

Judy, a pal and Gene in the Model T

The One And Only Yellow Model T Ford

We had a yellow Model T Ford, the likes of which I have never seen since! It had no top and what once must have been a backseat had been converted into a small truck bed. The Model T was used to carry equipment back-and-forth to the fields. Unbelievably, my Dad, who farmed all his life, never owned a pick-up truck. After the Model T bit the dust, he drove a small Chevrolet and carried a tool chest and an extra gas tank in the trunk which he used to fill up the equipment in the fields.

One awful winter's day when the weather was not fit for man or beast, one of us said, "Let's go to Ellis to bowl." (WaKeeney had yet to have a bowling alley.) It was cold, blustery, wet and ugly, but we bundled up and Mother, Dad, Gene and I piled into the front of the Model T Ford and off we tootled to the town of Ellis -15 miles away. We were freezing when we got there. Think about it this way ... it was like taking a golf cart minus the roof overland in a sleet storm.

As I remember the day, the weather was so bad that no one else was bowling. After having an extraordinary time of having the alley to ourselves, we scrambled back up into the Model T Ford for the cold and miserable return trip home. All in all it was a grand adventure.

***Aside:** During World War II Dad thought it his patriotic duty to donate the Model T to the war effort for spare parts. I still miss that Model T Ford.*

The Guacamole Green Hudson

When I was four years old, my folks bought a four-door, light green Hudson. Stick shift and all, it was a beautiful sight to behold. I first learned to drive in that car when I was 10 years old. At the end of one work day in the fields, there were three vehicles that needed to be driven the mile back to the house and only two drivers. Dad and Gene were trying

An Exciting Mode of Transportation

to figure out how to get the tractor, the wheat truck and the Hudson back to the house. The solution was obvious to me, so I chirped up, "I can drive the Hudson home." Though I don't remember the conversation between them, the next thing I knew I was the one driving the Hudson on the country road headed home. From that day on I could "drive". At the age of 14, when I was issued my first driver's license, I was so proud that I got to drive that very car - the guacamole green Hudson. It became a fantastic automobile for a teenager and all her friends.

The Big And Burly Harley-Davidson

My Dad had a big Harley-Davidson motorcycle which I thought was the coolest thing. He would take Gene and me to school on it. I would be in front of Dad and Gene would be holding on for dear life behind him. It didn't happen often, but enough times for me to remember that the motorcycle (with all three of us on it) would get caught in a rut on our terrible country road. Off we would tumble as the motorcycle careened on its side, out of control. We would pick ourselves up, dusted ourselves off, get back on and cruise home. When Mom saw our cuts, scrapes, and bruises - boy, would Dad get it!!!

Stranded

My big experience with the Harley came when Dad let me take my first solo run (sometime in my high school days). I successfully rode three miles east of the house where there were absolutely no houses and no people and tried to turn around. The engine died and I didn't have enough umph to kick start it, so I just sat there in the middle of the road on the Harley. I figured someone would eventually come by and help me or that Dad would miss me at home and come looking for me. After 10 or 15 minutes, sure enough, here came Dad in the Hudson. After he started it for me, I zipped home and I never drove it again.

Aside: Believe you me, that Harley was one big dude!

The Down And Dirty Work In The Fields

No Time For Dreaming...
But Someone Has To Do It

As soon as I was old enough, I began to work in the fields. An entry in my diary on May 16, 1945, reads: *worked on tractor for 2 ½ hours and earned 90 cents.* I was 11 at the time and I loved it!

When I first started to work in the fields, I would operate the old Wallis tractor (built 1920-1932) pulling a plow. Then one-way discs came along and were easier to use. Actually, working in the fields was probably a very boring job, but I never in my life have found anything really boring. As I sat on the hard metal seat (my feet barely reached the brake and the clutch pedals), I followed the furlough round and round the field, as the hot sun blazed and the dust swirled everywhere. I dreamed of buying my own land, imagined the travels I'd take, fantasized tall tales, wondered

Skipping Between The Raindrops 27

what I'd be when I grew up, and generally passed the time of day contemplating my future - and prayed for a cooling breeze.

When the fields and the ground were too wet, the one-ways would get clogged up. This meant stopping, getting off the tractor, reaching for the crowbar located on the one-way frame, and digging the dirt and mud away from the discs. *This was hard work!* Dawn to dusk was the order of the day and a shower in the Springhouse (whether the water flowed hot or cold) was a welcome respite.

A Wonderful Time of Year

The Money-Making Time Of The Year... Summer Wheat Harvest

Harvest lasted around two weeks - depending on rain and number of acres to be harvested. It was always an exciting event in late June and early July, and I looked forward to it every year - my favorite time. Dad hired a crew of two or three men and along with Gene the work day started at the crack of dawn. The crew did maintenance work on the machinery until around 10:00 am. This gave the wind time to dry the wheat from the moisture retained the night before. The machinery maintenance involved adjusting timing belts, greasing mechanical parts, gassing up and in general doing everything necessary to keep the equipment operational throughout the day.

Harvesting began in earnest around 10:00 am. The cutting stopped for lunch from 12 noon to 1:00 pm. Mother made it very clear that everyone had better be on time. Everyone came to the house and ate lunch inside around the dining room table. A typical meal consisted of fried chicken or *meatloaf*, mashed potatoes, cream gravy, fresh green beans, cucumbers and onions, sliced tomatoes, hot fresh homemade rolls with butter and a combination of honey and peanut butter. I really don't remember what we had for dessert, but I'm sure it tasted delicious because Mother was a fabulous baker.

See recipe from the Rinker kitchen at the back of the book!

There would be a sandwich snack at 4:00 pm. When I was too young to assist with the harvest, I would help Mother make ham and cheese sandwiches (mustard, no mayo), ham salad, beef spread, wiener spread, home-made cookies and lemonade to take to the fields. The work didn't stop - I would run and catch the bottom step of the moving combine, climb up and give the snack to Dad, Gene or to one of the hired hands; then I'd jump down. They would eat and drink while the combine blades chugged round and round. We'd wait for the truck drivers to return from unloading the wheat at the grain elevators in town, give them their snack and then head home.

Afternoons Were For My Love Of Reading

Judy bare-footed on the way upstairs to read

After we took the men their afternoon snack, I would head upstairs to my room, open my east facing windows to catch the afternoon breeze, lie flat on my stomach on the bed and read. My favorite magazines were

- *Redbook,*
- *McCall's,*
- *Good Housekeeping,*
- *Cosmopolitan,*
- *Saturday Evening Post,*
- *Reader's Digest,*
- my *Classics Illustrated* and
- my *Big-Little Books.*

My other book interests were eclectic; mystery, romance, adventure and historical novels were all included in my reading repertoire. Often, I would fall asleep and wake up in a pool of sweat. Since we had no air-conditioning at the time, the hundred degree plus temperatures tended to get us all down; the only saving grace was the wind. Of course with the windows open, we had to contend with the ever-present dust.

It was important to cut the wheat as late at night as possible since it was always wet in the mornings and there was always the fear of rain. Rain meant that you had to delay cutting until the fields and wheat dried. Too much rain would affect the quality of the kernels, and the weeds would grow making it harder to cut. This also lowered the price of the wheat because it would not be of a superior quality.

The crew completed work between 9:00 pm and 10:00 pm daily. The guys would head to their homes for supper, and Dad and Gene would shower in the Springhouse, come in and devour sandwiches, fruit and leftovers while sitting on stools at the counter in our small kitchen.

The Miscellaneous Memories Of Childhood

Mother And The County Engineer

Mother was a very strong-minded person who did not suffer fools gladly. She had a lifelong battle with the county engineers (she went through several) over our country road which, at the best of times, was none too good. The road graders would pile up dirt on one side of the road or the other which would narrow the road considerably. It made meeting a car challenging and passing one particularly exciting. The dust was horrendous, and since our house was fairly close to the road, it caught mounds of dirt as cars went by.

Mother hated it when, after a rain, the road would be in a fairly good and hard-packed condition when here would come the road grader creating plumes of dust! One day, Mother in a fit of rage, ran out to the road and stood in the middle of it with her arms out-stretched to make the grader stop. After giving the driver a piece of her mind, he finally lifted up the blade and left the road unturned for the length of our house and driveway. It was a beautiful act of civil defiance and I was so proud of Mother for doing it.

Later, we found out that the county engineer would give directives to grade the roads whether they needed it or not, so everyone could be paid for working! But after Mother's act of civil defiance, he informed the crew who came out on the Rinker road, to lift their blades as they came past our house.

Aside: *I always thought that was a wise decision on the county engineer's part.*

Mother And The Snake On The Prairie

One day while Dad worked in the fields, Mother walked to the mailbox about 225 feet away from the house to mail a letter. This had to be done before 11:00 am as the mail always came between 11:00 am and 11:30 am. Gene and I were little and were playing in the house. Suddenly, Mother burst through the back door and shouted, "Come on Gene, Come on Judy, get in the car. We're going to town." So off we scurried, jumped in the Hudson and raced five miles to town.

The doctor's office was downtown on the second floor of a building on Main Street. We ran up the stairs into a big open room, no receptionist, no waiting room, just the doctor. At this point, Mother announced to the doctor, "I've been bitten by a rattlesnake." What happened next is dim in my memory; however, Mother must have been treated by the doctor and we then drove back home. Mother fixed lunch, put us to bed for our afternoon naps and considered it all in a day's work! What and when Dad was told - I know not.

Mom and Mary on the Road

Mom's Trip To Central Park

Mom went with a group of her college friends on a camping trip to New York City sometime during the 1930's. The group traveled in a school bus and a car which Mom drove. They pitched tents alongside the road at night and cooked their meals on campfires. Upon arriving in New York City, they assembled their tents in Central Park. (Before Mom left, she cooked us a big turkey roaster full of ham and beans, and that's what we ate for two weeks!) Mom had a fantastic trip, but we sure did miss her - especially her cooking!

Trouble Pronouncing My "R's"

My speech impediment of not being able to pronounce my R's remained with me until my late 50s. One time as Mom ironed and I was just a little tike, I toddled over to her and pulled on the hem of her dress to get her attention. I said, "Momma, when I grow up, I'll do all the *wuk wound* the house." She laughed and thanked me for my kind thoughts.

Aside: Even as an adult upon making collect phone calls, I would pronounce my name as "Judy Winker," so I would always spell it for the operator. "That's Winker with an R, r-i-n-k-e-r, Winker."

The Clock On The Wall

Due to my inquisitive nature, my toddler years were spent driving my parents crazy.

It was my Mother who got the brunt of my zillion inquiring-mind questions every day. She would finally become totally exasperated and tell me, "Stop asking questions, Judith!" One of my most persistent questions tended to be "What time is it?" One day at the age of four, I stood in the kitchen staring at the octagonal 8 X 10 inch wall clock. I looked up at it and proudly announced, "It's four o'clock!" Mother was so surprised, as it was actually 4:00 pm, that she breathed a sigh of relief for now she would not have to answer "What time is it?" anymore.

Aside: Interestingly, I am still very much aware of time. I have dozens of watches and clocks (however no alarm clocks) and I still organize everything down to the minute.

The Ghost In The House

When I was little (I don't remember my age), but before I got promoted upstairs, I used to sleepwalk. One of my sleepwalking episodes took place one night about 2:30 am. I turned on, at full blast, the large console radio/record player in the living room. My folks were jarred awake and knew immediately the culprit of their untimely awakening; they went scurrying all around the house looking for me, but to no avail. Finally, they found me sitting on a stool in the walk-in closet of the master bedroom fast asleep. I remember nothing of this incident - only what's been told to me.

Story Telling Times

I wasn't sick very often as the Rinker family is a hardy bunch; but one of the nicest experiences when I was sick was being tucked into bed with a hot water bottle (either at my feet or on my chest or both), a cup of hot tea, a bowl of ice cream and, best of all, my Mother reading to me.

Mom read fairy tales, classics and poetry, and to this day I have maintained my love of poetry. I've always been puzzled why so many people dislike the rhyming of words. To me, it is music to my ears.

Homemade Lung Salve And Early To Bed

One thing I never got used to was the lung salve that went on my chest when I had a cold. Our local pharmacist made his own salve and it was truly potent stuff. *(I still have it in the original jar should anyone want some.)* The second thing I never got used to was going to bed early. Almost every night, until I entered high school, the lights went out by dark-thirty - sick or well. Dad had the say on this as we had a Delco generator in the garage which he would run a few hours an evening, but a little after dark - off it would go. Of course, we were lucky as most of our neighbors were still using their coal lamps.

I'm sure that going to bed so early in my young life led to my desire to "stay up late" which I have done the rest of my life. I still burn the midnight oil to midnight and beyond. In my younger days, however, I did like to sleep late (8:00 am -10:00 am), but as I have aged I find myself getting up earlier (6:30 am - 8:00 am*). At this early hour, I often look in the mirror and ask myself "Who is this person?"*

The Edge Of Death

WaKeeney had a city swimming pool off and on during the 1930-1940's. One summer day at the wee-age of five, I was at the pool. As I couldn't swim, I stayed mostly in the shallow end, but that day I walked around the deep end of the pool, slipped on the pavement and fell in. I will be forever grateful to that person or persons who jumped in and rescued me. It certainly taught me to have a healthy respect for water and I still have a genuine fear of drowning. I did, however, learn to swim, earned my life-saving certificate and taught swimming at the university level.

Aside: *In 1967 I was the last professor at Southwest Texas State University (now Texas State) who taught a summer swimming class in the San Marcos River. I would not be at all surprised if my students remember me telling them on the first day of class, "If you swim past my life-*

saving pole and float down the river - you're on your own." They could tell this was no trifling threat which certainly kept most in sight.

My Feeling For The Good $tuff

Later revelations will include my penchant for saving money, but earning money started at an early age. Mother loved to have her feet tickled and she would pay me (practically a babe-in-arms at the age of four) the princely sum of five cents an hour to "tickle her toes". This procedure probably lasted about five minutes but made everyone happy!

Gene and I were each given an allowance. I remember being given two dollars a week for helping the folks with chores out of which I faithfully tried to save one dollar. Although I have never been particularly enamored with money and I've never worked only for money, I've always loved what I've done to make money. In my mind's eye, my big goal in life was to become a millionaire. Saving 10% to 20% of what I earned along the way turned out to be a doable task. However, it certainly helped being single and usually sharing expenses with one or two others. I still consider it a miracle that I was able to save anything since, after teaching and coaching for 18 years (13 at the University level), my top salary was $13,000. At the guest ranch I co-owned and ran for 27 years, the staff for the first 20 of those years made more than I did!

Aside: *It truly is a puzzlement to me that I ever reached my goal. However, the sale of the guest ranch certainly contributed to this achievement.*

An Affinity For The Land And The Land Deal Of The Decade

My love and affection for the vast prairies of Western Kansas manifested in me the desire to own my own land. Since I just spent my allowance for incidentals like movies, popcorn, Green Rivers (a wonderful beverage concoction at the local soda fountain-bakery), it was not too difficult to save enough to begin to purchase land from my Dad at the going rate of $35 an acre. Eventually, I bought 50 acres.

Unfortunately, there were no records (except for my checks) of these great and major transactions. When I became interested in placing my feet on these 50 acres, there was no defined 50 acre tract for me to do so. I did get paid the crop income from the "south 40" (50 acres) after Mother prodded Dad to make sure I didn't get short-changed.

Years later, when wills and trusts were being made, it became apparent that it was going to be too difficult to give me a deed to my acreage. The land would have to be surveyed, and most of the land in our county is calculated by 1/4, 1/2 and 1 section increments. Mother finally convinced us that the simplest solution would be for Dad just to buy the land back from me. He did, but I have no recollection of what price we decided was fair. I paid for the land, and later Dad would pay me for the crop production which was just turning the money around. The problem was that I ended up without having anything concrete to show for all my "savings".

Aside: *However, in looking back on it, I believe it to be one of the greatest land frauds in history.*

Gene and Judy – Here Comes Double Trouble

Brotherly Love - My Hero And My Cohort In Crime

First Name Basis

Gene always called our folks by their first names, Frank and Hermena. I never did know exactly why he did that, but maybe due to his early years of hearing my parents and their friends calling each other by their first names, he just picked it up. I always thought it to be unusual! (*Actually, strange!!*) Although I never called our parents by their first names, I did call all their friends by their first names. I was probably just imitating what Gene did. Once in a while, it did get a little sticky as Mother's best friend, Mary Harries, whom she met as a fellow high school teacher in the mid-1920's and with whom she roomed at the teacherage, was my high school typing teacher. I always had to stop and think to call her Mrs. Harries and not Mary.

Swinging High

We had a cloth hammock which we set up between two trees in our front yard. We could actually set up another one between a third tree when we were so inclined. One day I got to swinging too high and fell out on the grass and broke my collarbone. I had to stay home from school for several days as well as to wear a most uncomfortable brace. I was quite proud of being able to say that I broke my collar bone by falling out of a hammock; not everyone could claim that distinction. I have always felt that it was not my fault, as Gene was swinging me. I'm sure, however, that I was imploring him to swing me higher and higher. I feel certain that he was scolded for following my directions!

Judy and the infamous hammock

Just Shoot Me

Gene and I had, as most children do, a fascination with guns. One of the best Christmas presents we ever received was the Christmas morning my Mom reached under her bed and pulled out two BB guns - one for me and one for Gene. We were in heaven. However, when we misbehaved, the guns disappeared and had to be earned back.

One such occasion happened one day when Gene and I were out in the front yard playing.

"Mama, I'm Innocent!"

He wanted to shoot his BB gun in the direction where I was standing. When I refused to move, he just pointed the gun in my direction and fired. Needless to say, I got pummeled with a BB and I immediately ran wailing into the kitchen, where Mom was working, to tattle on him. She rushed outdoors giving us a piece of her mind. Gene stoically held his ground, gun in hand, and patiently explained to Mom that it was all my fault. He wanted to shoot where I was standing. Since I wouldn't move, it was my fault that I got hit with a BB that he fired. The result of this foray was the disappearance of the guns for several weeks.

The Tale Of The Bruised Buttocks

One day as I played soldier with my BB gun on my shoulder marching up and down on our only sidewalk; Mom called me into the porch. I marched in, having no idea what she might want. Upon arriving inside, Mom asked me if I had been smoking. I couldn't imagine where she'd get that idea; but my answer was obviously not the right one as the next thing I knew, I was getting a few whacks with the BB gun against my backside.

I did receive quite a few spankings as a child since I was not only an ornery cuss but also a really stubborn one. Both Gene and I would try Mom's patience to the hilt. Most of the spankings were administered with a hand, but we did get the occasional butt of the BB gun or Dad's shaving strap. Since I was well padded, it never hurt for long, and I can honestly say I'm not any worse for any of the spankings. And there was always a reason for the spankings: smoking, lying, acting up in public or not doing what was asked. The spankings did not happen that often, were always administered on the backside, and were reasonably brief. The tears never lasted too long.

Gone Fishing

One summer day, there was no work in the fields since it had rained the night before, so Dad dropped Gene and me off at Mong's pond to go fishing. The pond was about three miles from home as the crow flies. We each had a bamboo cane pole. For several hours we sat on the bank in the hot sun with nary a bite or a sight of a fish. At noon, we ate our sack lunches and started fishing again. Around 2:00 pm, Gene got deathly sick, *probably sunstroke!* Well, Dad wasn't picking us up until around 4:00 pm to 5:00 pm, so I found a shade tree for Gene to rest under and I began hiking to the nearest house about 1/2 mile away. When I got there no one was home, but the house was unlocked, so I went in and searched for a phone. Luckily, they had one, and I called the folks to come get us as Gene was sick. He was fine once we got home and he was administered ice packs, food and water! *Neither one of us had a nibble all day; therefore, my first day of fishing was also my last!*

Scarred For Life

I have two scars, one from my eighth grade light bulb incident (more on this later) and another from an excursion with Gene.

We were playing in the wheat field and decided it was time for a break. There was a barbed wire fence on the side of the barn next to the wheat field with a large, heavy barbed wire gate. To get back to the house we had to go through this gate. Gene told me to unfasten and lift the gate up while it was being opened. I unfastened it, but I didn't feel like following his directive to hold it up, so I let the gate drop to the ground at which time the barbed wire barbs ripped down my arm creating a bleeding gash from my elbow to my wrist.

I raced to the house, yelling at the top of my lungs that I was bleeding to death. I'm certain that Mom thought I was dying, but she just pulled the skin together, threw on a disinfectant (probably merthiolate which we used for everything) and band-aided it together. About that time, Gene meandered in to face Mom's wrath. "What did you do to Judith?" asked Mom. His unruffled response was "I told her to hold up the gate and she didn't do it."

Aside: To this day I have a beautiful scar (lessened by age) on my right arm.

The Games We Played Down On The Farm

Fun With Pocket Knives

Kids growing up in the country learned to entertain themselves. We played many games both indoors and out and Mumbly-Peg was one of my favorites. You took your pocket knife, drew a 5 to 6 foot diameter circle in the dirt and threw the knife so it would stick upright. Then you would mark that section off. The object of the game was to stick your knife in the smallest section of the circle to win.

The Homemade High Jump

Gene and I built a high jump stand in the pasture near the barn. I don't think we had anything to land on except dirt. Needless to say, I never got very good, but Gene developed into an excellent high jumper.

The Hoopsters

Dad put a basketball hoop (no netting) up on the front of the barn where it got hundreds of hours of action. The dirt was fairly level so bouncing the ball wasn't too difficult. Gene and I played 21 and H-O-R-S-E for hours-on-end. Basketball became one of my favorite sports.

Aerial Tennis

During the sixth grade when I started playing tennis, I used the back of the barn for practice. The back side didn't have so many protuberances although the ground was more of a challenge. Thus, I became very proficient at short aerial volleys. All my practicing came in handy when I played on the high school tennis team.

Baseball In The Front Yard

We all played baseball and catch a lot too. Mom, Dad, Gene and I would stand out in the middle of our circle drive to throw, pitch and bat a baseball, often until it got so dark that we couldn't see the ball anymore. In the winter, Dad and I would go to the barn and climb up the very difficult, toe-grip ladder on the workshop wall to get up to the haymow.

We would then throw a baseball back-and-forth by the dim illumination of a single light bulb. It was all great fun!

Is This Baseball or What?

Left Or Right Handed?

Indoors, I played table tennis on the concrete wall and floor in the basement where I challenged my left hand against my right hand. Jacks, another one of my favorite games, was played on the linoleum floor in the hallway adjacent to the dining room. Again, I played my left hand against my right hand. *Many times it has been advantageous to be ambidextrous and playing against myself, I always won!*

We Were All Sharks

At some point, the Boy Scout house was undergoing remodeling and we were asked to store the pool table. We had the table in the basement for several years before they needed it back. Then we bought a table tennis table which I still have. It must be around 75 years old by now. Both tables endured much use through the years and we all became pros.

The Games We Played In Town

Hide And Seek And Icebox

Playing in town was always a real thrill for me. Living on the farm, my playmate choices were Gene, Dianne, my folks or friends who had been invited out. In town, the possibilities were endless. I remember vividly the night I stayed with my friend Kathleen. She had an older sister and a younger sister (who later became my secretary when I was teaching at Fort Hays State University in Hays, Kansas). Verna Lou, another classmate, lived two houses down and another friend Malcolm lived across the street. Before the sun went down, there were a whole kit and caboodle of us playing hide and seek around the block. As it got darker, we switched to icebox - one of my favorite games (although I can't quite remember what it was all about). I thought it was a blast as most often "down on the farm" I would end up playing by myself or with Gene.

The Game Of Life – Bridge

Bridge Is The Love Of My Life

The earliest mention of playing bridge is notated in my diary on April 27, 1945, when I was 11 years young: *Went to school in the Model T Ford again this morning. Got out early and came home in the rain. Played bridge after supper.* I obviously had been playing for some time as the entry sounds pretty matter-of-fact. It also means Gene was home as we were always a foursome. He would have been 14 at the time.

In various and sundry entries I made the playing of bridge seem like an everyday occurrence, and in my memory

I believe that it was. I can't remember the exact time or age when I first learned to play, but I think I caught on very quickly with my brother, my Mother and my Dad all giving me instructions. It was a situation of "learn or go to bed!" *And man, I never wanted to go to bed!*

Champions

Both of the folks were champions of the "early to bed" school of thought, so if the cards were really bad, we never continued playing past 10:00 pm. If things were going well, we got to play a while longer. Gene most frequently played with Mother and I was normally Dad's partner. Gene, Dianne and I all played cards "left-handed" which we must have picked up from Dad as Mother played "right-handed". Really have no idea why we all took after Dad but we did!

The Card Shark Kids – Gene, Dianne, Judy

My Dad, The Card-Shark

Everyone, most of all Mother, accused Dad of being lucky at cards. And it was true to a great extent. My Dad could squeeze, finesse and manipulate until his opponents believed that he would make his bid, no matter what. Even as a child I can remember Dad bidding his perpetual "Three No Trump". He was apt to bid it with or without any help from his partner. Almost always he really didn't have enough count to make the bid, but more times than not he would. This always infuriated Mother who would say, "Frank, do you always have to bid 'Three No Trump'?" Dad would just grin sheepishly and go on his merry way.

I noticed through the years that Dad made no attempt to discourage this belief that he was "lucky at cards," and eventually I began to realize that he used this feeling/belief as a weapon against his opponents. They would never know whether he was bluffing or really had the cards, and even when he didn't, he continued his bluff. He would take trick after trick with his low cards while his opponents saved their high cards, until they realized it was too late for them to have any value. Nothing delighted Dad more than when this happened. I, too, feel as if I am really lucky at cards, and I know that I acquired this attribute from my Dad. It does affect one's play to believe that you will always win, and what's more, it certainly does affect your opponent's attitude!

Mom's Perspective: Bad Cards = BEDTIME

I can remember many times when Mother's cards were so bad that she would throw them down on the table and announce with disgust "I quit!". Sometimes, we could coax her into another hand; and if she were dealt a really good one, we would be allowed to stay up for a little while longer. If her cards were not good, the game was usually over for the evening and *time for bed.*

Hooked On Smokin'

Pilfering Smokes

My folks played in two bridge groups, Friday Night Bridge Club and Saturday Night Bridge Club. The clubs met on alternate weeks; although there were some of the same couples each night, there were at least 50% different couples. Each couple hosted and after everyone had their turn, the rotation started over again. They all came dressed up, the men in suits and ties and the women in fancy dresses and snazzy jewelry. The best china and silver came out for the evening *hors d'oeuvres*.

* *See recipes from the Childs and Rinker kitchens at the back of the book!*

All Dressed-Up for Bridge

    To the best of my recollection no one in either group smoked, but packages of cigarettes were placed on each table: Camels, Lucky Strikes and Chesterfields. Gene and I were relegated to our rooms upstairs, but we could hear all the excitement and the laughter taking place downstairs.

What Were We Thinking?

    Gene and I would set our alarms for 5:30 am the next morning; when we were buzzed awake, we would get dressed, sneak downstairs to the living room and slip two or three cigarettes out of each open package. This might give us a total of 10 to 15 cigarettes. Then, we would hightail it out to the back of the barn where the plows and one-ways were parked for the winter. We would store the cigarettes unprotected from the elements among various tool chests on the machinery. We knew no one would use the tool chests until late spring.

Whenever we had a chance, we would go out and have a smoke. You can imagine how strong the cigarettes became over the course of the next three to six months until the next party rolled around. Of course, the cigarettes did have to be gone before Dad began to check the equipment for use in the spring.

Aside: I'm convinced to this day that one of the reasons I never took to smoking seriously was because of the vile and rancid cigarettes Gene and I smoked those many years ago.

Am I Crazy? Or What?

And speaking of cigarettes, I used to get so desperate for a smoke that I would light up paper straws! These were quite terrible. One day during a grade school lunch hour, I hiked downtown 4 or 5 blocks to get a dime hamburger at the Bon Ton Cafe. As I was coming out of the café, I spied a cigarette butt in the gutter. Although I don't remember where I got a match, I do remember smoking the butt! No wonder smoking never appealed much to me as I got older. *I wasn't exactly smoking the pick of the leaves.* I was permanently cured of smoking at the age of 22 when I was seated next to a smoker on a Pan American flight from San Francisco to Melbourne for the Olympics. He was kind enough to ask me if I cared if he smoked and I was nice enough to say "No problem". What was I thinking? *Boy, was that a mistake!!!* About 15 hours later I was completely nauseated.

Aside: Since I traveled quite a bit, there was no one happier than I when smoking was banned from airplanes.

I Came To My Senses

I think my experiences with smoking were just something daring to do because it was "forbidden". As an adult, I never did take up smoking as a full-time vice. I will confess to smoking a cigarette or two now and then and an occasional pipe during my college days. At the time, nothing would have made me happier than to have smoking banned in public places so I didn't have to breathe other people's follies. But, on the other hand, I certainly wouldn't want to have relinquished all my childhood smoking escapades.

Aside: The above was written in the beginning stages of this book in 1974 so the following will show how much people and times can and do change. Who would believe in their wildest dreams that Texas would ban smoking in most public buildings - even bars. Just goes to show you what is possible.

The Social Graces And Gatherings Of The Time

Civility Starts At Home

Mother and Dad did have lots of company. Friends would drop by, sometimes for afternoon chatter, sometimes for dinner, and sometimes for relaxation. What I remember most vividly were the conversations. We all talked about everything: the war, politics, religion, people and ideas. Through it all no one could tell who was a Democrat or a Republican, who was a Presbyterian, a Catholic or an atheist. I never knew until years later which political party my parents belonged to. We discussed ideas and no one got hot under the collar, felt left out or was too verbally abused.

Learning The Social Graces

My penchant for parties goes back as far as I can remember. When I was in early grade school, my Mother would arrange a dinner party for the entire grade school faculty. I extended an invitation to each female teacher and to a friend. We would sit at bridge (card) tables complete with linen tablecloths, linen napkins, sterling silverware and our best china and crystal. Four tables would be arranged throughout the living room with about 16 or so of us. I would, of course, dress up in my Sunday best (knowing me, I'm sure this was not my favorite part of the evening). The Rinkers would then play host to all the teachers, except for Mr. Noel, the principal, the only male teacher in grade school.

Guests socializing in the Rinker living room with Mom on right

In looking back, I am so grateful to my folks, probably mostly my Mother, for providing me with the social graces and an air of comfort and confidence that I gained on such occasions. To this day, I feel that I wouldn't get overly nervous about entertaining the Queen of England or any other world dignitary. *After all, I helped entertain the entire faculty of the WaKeeney grade school at the age of six!*

We probably hosted these "first of school year dinners" many times through my grade school days, but I'll never forget the excitement of the first one. A current observation is that I can't believe any of this actually took place. It is difficult to imagine anything like this happening in this day and age. In point of fact, I've never been too sure how usual it was even back then. However, since my Mother had taught in the local high school, she knew many of the teachers so I imagine that familiarity helped to smooth the way for such a social gathering.

The Spoiled Brat At My Birthday Party Was Me

I have loved parties and partying from my earliest days and some of my best memories are celebrating my family's birthdays. One such memory involves my Mother putting *mushrooms* in the gravy for my birthday dinner. She had never done that before, and she thought it would be a *special treat*. Well, I raised holy hell because, first of all, I didn't like mushrooms (*did anyone even know that?*) and secondly, I hadn't requested them. Yet, I did look forward to the mouth-watering *Chocolate Beet Cake* that Mom had prepared for my birthday.

* See recipes from the Rinker kitchen at the back of the book!

Skipping Between The Raindrops

Judy and Skippy Celebrating

No-Girls-Allowed Birthday Party For Gene

And then, there was one of Gene's birthday parties which, I was informed, was to be for boys only. I was so devastated that I talked Mother into convincing Gene to let me partake of the hotdog phase of the party. On this particular party day, the wind was blowing ferociously (it always blew so we're talking about intensity here). I was upstairs in my room and decided it was time to come down for the feasting festivities. I opened the upstairs door and started my descent at which point the wind blew the door shut behind me. I was knocked down the whole flight of 15 stairs! Although feeling more hurt than truly injured, the tumble bruised my pride to the extent that I did not attend the wiener roast. *Needless to say, I was heartbroken.*

Dianne's Fifth Birthday Party Arrives

On June 5, 1945, I wrote in my diary: *Had Dianne's birthday party tonight. Tomorrow is really her birthday but Mother had to go to a supper so we're having it tonight.* My June 6 entry reads: *Today is really Dianne's birthday but we had a party yesterday!* Dianne would have been five and I was 11 at the time.

The Crossing Of The Eyes

I used to love to cross my eyes, and I could "single cross" and "double cross" them at will. At one of the birthday parties, I gave all the guests a treat by "double crossing" them. Everyone, except for my Mother, laughed uproariously. Mother was entreating me to stop. She said, "What if your eyes would stay that way?" *I'll have to admit that would have been a catastrophe.* I gradually grew out of this exhibitionist stage.

The Radio Waves Saved The Days And Nights

Popcorn, Ice Cream, WWII And Boxing

In the 1940's the radio was our slender thread which connected us to the rest of the world. Whole evenings were reserved for *Your Hit Parade*, Jack Benny, *Intersanctum* and *The Shadow*. After listening, we would almost always have either popcorn or ice cream, and at 9:00 pm (dark-thirty) we would all go to bed as Dad would turn off the Delco generator. It was all great fun and oh, so innocent!

I vividly remember two particular radio incidents. The first was when we came home after church on Sunday, December 7, 1941 to the news that the Japanese had bombed Pearl Harbor. The second was the *Joe Louis - Jersey Joe Walcott* boxing match. I loved the boxing matches as we all listened avidly and reacted to the description of each body blow.

The Love Of Boxing Dies

Eventually, two things killed my enthusiasm for boxing. One was a bout with a friend at Girl Scouts (more on this later), and the second was attending my first "live" fight at the 1956 Melbourne Olympics in Australia. I was so excited to see a boxing match in living color that I could hardly wait to get to the venue. But when the boxing matches started, and I saw each body blow, many centered on the head (there was no headgear back then), it was a far different sport from when all this was described in detail over the radio. Seeing it was like entering another world. I left the boxing arena before the end of the matches, and I've never seen or listened to another fight. *There must be better ways to 1) earn a living and 2) take out one's aggressions than boxing!*

In Good Times And Bad
Fostering The Ties That Bind

Harmonic Sing-A-Longs

One of the most wonderful things in my life growing up was the music. Mother played a "mean" piano; with her share of the wheat money in the 1930's, she bought a baby grand piano. My sister, Dianne, now has Mother's piano and plays it frequently. Many evenings, if we weren't playing bridge, we had sing-a-longs. As Dad sat in the rocking chair claiming he couldn't sing, the rest of us gathered around the piano with me sitting to the right of Mom on the piano bench, not too close as she needed room to "tickle-the-ivories," and the rest standing close behind. We sang every genre of songs with Dianne singing melody, Mom singing harmony and Gene and I filling in between the notes. Any night with guests could end with these musical moments. Several of the men in my folks' social groups had tremendous voices, and it was always a special treat to hear them letting go.

**Piano, Cornet and Saxophone Jam Session
starring Judy, Mom and Dianne**

Contributions To The War Effort Were Made Personal

Sometime during World War II (1941-1945), an entrepreneur remodeled an empty downtown building into a small four to six lane bowling alley. At this time, this was the nearest bowling alley to Walker Army Airfield 50 miles to the east of WaKeeney. The flyers would hitch-hike to town for entertainment along US 40 (now Interstate 70). We met some of the flyers while bowling, and Mom invited them out to the farm for dinner. Eventually, several would just hitch-hike out to the farm for games, good food, enlightening conversation and sing-a-longs.

Several of the fellows remained our friends for life. I wrote to them with V-Mail (Victory Mail) letters during the war; one who was from New Jersey showed my sister the sights of New York many years later. And speaking of mail, at the ages of seven to eleven, I wrote letters to many of the soldiers, sailors and flyers during the war and received bukoos of V-mails back.

V-mail correspondence was on small letter sheets, 7" x 9", which would go through mail censors before being photographed and transported as thumbnail-sized images in negative microfilm. Upon arrival at their destination, the negatives would be printed. The final print was 60% of the original document's size, creating a sheet 4" x 5". According to the National Postal Museum, "V-mail ensured that thousands of tons of shipping space could be reserved for war materials."

The Major Calamity That Burned Me Up

I had a whole trunk of these letters plus dozens of what were called *Big-Little Books* and *Classics Illustrated* comic magazines stored in what we called the North Room. This room, adjacent to my bedroom, overflowed with many of my prized possessions. One day, in the late 1940's, I came home from school to find all my North Room treasures gone. I cried and carried on while Dad explained to me that he had burned all my letters and my *Big-Little Books* and my *Classics Illustrated* because he was afraid the floor/ceiling was going to collapse.

Aside: I never thought to ask Mother if she knew he was going to destroy them, as I'd like to think she wouldn't have let him do it! Of course, I'm sure that now both letters and books would be very valuable. Boo-hoo, I'm still crying about it!

The Etiquette Of Making Social Calls

Visits To My Wonderful Neighbors

I loved visiting the neighbors because everyone was so different - and I loved all the diversity. Most had no electricity, no indoor plumbing; most had hand-operated water pumps in the kitchen, different kinds of stoves, comfy old furniture and tasty ethnic foods. It was all very intriguing. My modes of transportation to visit my neighbors were walking, pedaling my bike or riding Tarzan, my black and white pony. My horsemanship left a lot to be desired; inevitably I got bucked off at the furthest point from the house. *Oh God, how I hated that horse.* I would have to walk home, or if I were lucky, I'd be in the yard of a neighbor who I then had an excuse to visit. Sometimes, they would drive me home or call my folks to come after me. And fortunately, Tarzan was always waiting at home to greet me.

Visiting Mrs. Rasek

Mrs. Rasek lived about two miles southwest of our house. Sometimes I went with Mother by car, and sometimes I pedaled my bike over. I loved to visit her as her house was really different from ours. She was Bohemian (whatever that was), and she made the best kolaches (pastry around fruit filling) on her coal oil stove. Having no electricity, she used coal oil lamps for lighting which I found very intriguing, especially since Mother warned me not to read by them as I would ruin my eyesight. Of course, she never explained to me why Mrs. Rasek didn't ruin her eyesight.

Dinner Invitations - New Taste Introductions

Late one summer afternoon, I rode Tarzan to the neighbor's farm about two miles southeast of our house. They invited me to supper and I was delighted to accept. I don't remember what was served except for one main dish. A large bowl of mashed potatoes was passed around; since this was one of my favorite foods (*still is*), I took a hefty portion. When I took the first bite, I thought I'd die because it had a strange and awful taste. I couldn't imagine what it was. Trying not to gag, I nonchalantly asked, "What am I eating?" "Mashed turnips" was the reply. I managed to politely consume the mound on my plate. I had never had turnips before and have never had them since!!!

Another time I rode to the neighbors a mile straight south through the wheat fields and pastures. From my house they could only be reached by walking or by pony. They lived in a two-story house with numerous out-buildings. Two of the sons were in my brother's class in high school (not twins), and one of the younger sons was in my high school class. One night we sat down to a supper of bread with milk poured over it. This was a meal I had never had before or since. Life was always presenting new tastes to me.

Visiting Roy And Esther
Slumber Party On The Floor

Two of the most interesting neighbors to visit were my Dad's half-brother Roy and his wife Esther. They were "summer farmers" as they lived winters in apartment houses in Denver and Kansas City; in the summers they lived in the Deines apartments in WaKeeney. Roy would drive out to the farm every day, and Esther would bring the noon meal to be served in the old railroad box car which was located near the out-buildings. There was an old cook stove, table and benches in the box car, but no water, electricity or telephone. The outhouse was behind the box car.

Their farm, only a quarter-mile east of our house, was an easy bike ride and I spent many an hour "living a different life" there. Sometimes when the men worked late, Esther would come out to bring another meal. In the evenings, a sudden thunderstorm might come up, and the road would become impossible for bike or car transport. After the rain, I would go outdoors and shout across the field to my folks informing them that I was staying all night. Then, the blankets would come out and be thrown on the floor. Whoever was there at the time would lie down in their clothes and sleep on the blankets – what fun!

Visiting The Spenas

Many happy hours were spent at the Spena family home. Freda, Glen and their daughter LaQuita, who was Gene's age, lived about one and one-half miles north of us on another unpaved county road. Biking or riding Tarzan was an easy trek. Sometimes when I stopped by for a visit, no one would be home. Doors were not locked so I thought nothing of picking up the mail from their mailbox, taking it into their house, and reading the newspaper. If they had not returned by that time, I left a note and headed for home.

Other times I would be sitting in the rocking chair in the kitchen when I heard their vehicle drive in. I would run and hide, but when Freda opened the door her first words would be "Hi Judd. Where are you?" *(She called me Judd her entire life.)* For years I wondered how she knew I was there (especially with Tarzan usually already home). Finally, she told me that when I ran to hide, I always left the rocking chair rocking.

Where's Judd?

On one occasion Gene and I were roaming around the Spenas' house since we had come to visit and no one was home. When the Spenas walked in, Gene was in the kitchen and he was asked, "Where's Judd?" His response was "She's in the attic". They all broke out laughing as they expected me to fall through the ceiling at any moment because there was no flooring, just cross-timbers. Luckily I made it down safely.

Aside: I have no recollection of this event. LaQuita reminded me of this incident when I spoke to her in 2020 about some of my escapades.

Before electricity, their house was lit by gas lamps fueled by white gas and kerosene lamps which were used to read by at the kitchen table. LaQuita told me there was no "reading in bed" during those 1930 days as one might end up on fire. She obviously held to this life-threatening notion because in 1944 she wrote in my autograph book:

*Dear Judy,
Two little gremlins
dressed in green,
Started to Harvard in a
flying machine,
Up came a storm and down
they fell
Instead of going to
Harvard they went to _____.
Now, don't get excited,
don't get pale,
Instead of going to
Harvard
They went to Yale.
Love, LaQuita
(Loot - her nickname)*

LaQuita, Friend Forever

The Coming Of REA

Under President Franklin Delano Roosevelt, the Rural Electrification Act of 1936 (REA) was created to bring electricity to rural areas. At this time, only 10% of farms in the USA had electric power because the cost to get electricity to rural areas was too expensive. It wasn't until 1945 that electricity finally came to our county via the Western Cooperative Electric Association, and the lives of the people in the rural communities changed – all for the better.

My Fascination With Coal Oil

The Spenas' coal oil stove fascinated me. It had four burners and no built-in oven. If you needed to bake something, there was a 14"L x 10"W X 10"H tin box with two interior racks that would be placed over one of the burners. There was really no way to adequately adjust the temperature so whatever was to be baked was done "by guess, by golly!" Freda was a really good cook, and I can remember her *Burnt Sugar Cake* which was absolutely delicious. She also coated the bacon with flour before frying it, which was unusual but very good. How she did all this on a coal oil stove was a mystery to me.

* See recipe from the Spena kitchen at the back of the book!

Vocabulary Lessons By Glen (Mr. Spena)

Glen raised both wheat and cattle. Their farm was on the southern edge of rolling hills and pasture land which went to the north many miles whereas my Dad's wheat fields to the south were flat and treeless. Glen swore like a trooper, and I was always captivated hearing some of the language he used. As my Dad seldom swore, Glen helped me with my extra-curricular vocabulary education.

Friends For Life

I have remained friends with the Spenas my whole life. Glen passed away in 1977. A few years later, Freda and I tootled around England, Ireland and Wales for several weeks. We rented an orange Volkswagen, stayed in bed and breakfasts, absorbed the local color and all-in-all had a fabulous time. She passed away in 2004. LaQuita and her husband, Harlen, built a house near her parents' former homestead. Harlen passed away in 2015 and LaQuita lived in WaKeeney until 2018 at which time she went to live with her son in Denver. We're still friends and discuss the affairs of the world via telephone.

The Best Of Summer Fun
Concerts, Movies & Hixson's Pond

Most regular social events such as club meetings, church gatherings and choir practices were suspended during the summer farming season. In their place were the weekly band concerts, the double-feature movies and social picnics.

Catching Fireflies

We would go to town with our parents on Saturday nights for the free band concerts in the city park. High school band members as well as alums played in the band. As the adults sat on metal chairs around the bandstand, the kids ran all around the park catching fireflies. As we kids advanced into high school, many of us also played in the summer band, and we in turn watched the younger kids run around and catch fireflies just as we had done years before.

The Movies - Food

Later, all the kids would run across the street from the park to the Kelly Theater for a double feature. Going to the movies was a real "happening" back then. Early on, the movies cost five cents for children 12 and under and 10 cents for adults. Then the cost went to 10 cents and 15 cents respectively. After paying the admission, everyone flocked around the concession stand which consisted of nickel and dime popcorn, milk duds, red-licorice, Raisinets, candy bars, Grapette, Pepsi, Coke, Mountain Dew, Root Beer, Orange, 7-Up and fountain sodas.

Aside: No one had ever heard of Dr Pepper in our neck of the woods at that time.

The Movies - Fun

Then we would file into the theater which had hardback seats and into a world of romance and adventure. First, there was a drawing with someone in the audience winning a free movie ticket. There was a small cash award which always seemed like a fortune to us. Next, we played several games of Bingo with prizes followed by a sing-a-along. This was accomplished by having the words and musical notes displayed on the screen with a bouncing ball showing us how to sing the tune. Everyone in the theater participated and a great time was had by all.

The Movies - Serial

Best of all was the serial which usually ran for 12 to 13 weeks - just the length of the summer. Of course, it was a big

Skipping Between The Raindrops 75

selling point when we asked our parents if we could go to the movies; we couldn't possibly miss an episode of the serial. The one I'll always remember was *The Scorpion*. It started with a giant scorpion displayed across the screen. None of us had ever seen a live scorpion, so it was quite impressive as well as scary to see the image of one multiplied about 100 times right there in front of us.

Aside: *This prepared me for the zillions of scorpions I have encountered during my life in Texas.*

The Movies - Main Features And Westerns

Then, we'd get to the "main feature" which was usually a first run movie - several months late. We knew all the main actors and actresses of the time: Clark Gable, Betty Grable, Jeanne Crain, Dana Andrews, Jimmy Cagney, Liz Taylor, June Allyson, Jimmy Stewart and Gary Cooper etc. But then the *crème de la crème* was left for last. Every Saturday night we got to see our favorite Western actors: Gene Autry, Roy Rogers, Dale Evans, Jack Palance, Smiley, Sons of the Pioneers, Don "Red" Barry and my favorite, Hopalong Cassidy, in a rip-roaring Western saga. Polishing off the evening with a stirring cowboy movie was like experiencing nirvana every week.

The Winter Movie Matinees

Through grade school during winter months our family would go to the 3:00 pm Sunday matinees at the Kelly Theater. It was always a family movie, and many other parents were there with their children. It was a far cry from the Saturday night melees which were predominately children.

In 1945, I wrote in my diary: *Saw Song of Bernadette with Jennifer Jones. It was wonderfully acted and good.*

On May 2, 1948 I wrote in my diary after seeing *Treasure of the Sierra Madre: It was sort of unusual.* Now, it is considered a classic.

Fun At Hixson's Pond

The Hixsons, members of the Saturday Night Bridge Club, invited the other six to eight couples and all their children to gather every summer Sunday evening at 5:30 pm to their pond for a picnic. Water was scarce in Western Kansas so it was a treat to go to a lake (even one without trees).

Running Wild

We, the eight to ten of us kids, would run down to the pond, dip our feet into the water, look for crawdads and just have a good time. The adults, in the meantime, sat visiting and exchanging gossip. Around sunset we would all gather; the adults on lawn chairs and the kids sitting cross-legged on the ground, to feast on the delicious goodies from the overflowing picnic baskets.

In The Twilight Of The Evening

Giant cumulus clouds billowed in the azure blue sky, and the sun exploded in a blaze of glory as it went down over the ever-expanding, treeless prairie. As the sun disappeared beyond the endless horizon, a small campfire was built and the group sat encircling it. As darkness fell, I could picture cowboys camped along the trail sipping coffee around their campfire, singing mournful ballads and listening to the sounds of grazing cattle, howling coyotes and rustling grass.

Wonderful Memories

I looked forward to, and still vividly remember, the sights and sounds of each Sunday night when our group, many with wonderful voices, sat around the campfire and harmonized various popular songs of the day: "In the Evening by the Moonlight," "Bicycle Built for Two," "Yankee Doodle Dandy," "Streets of Laredo," "Swing Low, Sweet Chariot," "Give My Regards to Broadway," "Home on the Range" (the Kansas state song) and dozens more.

Roasting Marshmallows

When voices played out, marshmallows were roasted over the embers and eaten with sticky fingers, and then the evening ended with a few more songs. In my mind, I can still picture the campfire scene at Hixson's pond on those beautiful Sunday evenings a lifetime ago.

Aside: There is nothing so memorable as a group of friends sitting around a campfire in the dark of night, away from civilization, harmonizing the evening away.

Never Let It Go

The culmination of the evening would take place in the car with Dad driving down the dark, lonely road home, Mother sitting in the front seat beside him, the kids in the back seat with me leaning up and asking Mother a thousand questions probably about some gossip I overheard among the grown-ups. And yes, I received the normal response from Mother. After answering several questions, she would say, "Judith, do not ask another question!" *That was not the first or the last time that I had received that response. I was a very inquisitive kid!*

Part II

My Grade School Debut

Learning The Ropes

The Red Brick Haven

Our grade school was a rectangular, two-story, red brick building with a basement. The basement consisted of the only restrooms for the entire building, the gym and the junior high shop. There were large concrete steps leading down onto the gym floor and a side room for the shop classes. The first floor contained classrooms for grades one through five. The second floor housed the principal's office, classrooms for grades six through eight, a large music/meeting room with a stage and a home economics sewing room.

Skipping Between The Raindrops 81

My Traumatic First Day Of School

My first day of school in first grade was very traumatic for me. I can still remember the incident as if it were yesterday. I was made aware of two HUGE failings that cut me to the core.

Wonderful Mrs. Springer

My first grade teacher was Mrs. Bessie Springer. She treated each one of her 30 plus pupils as equals with firmness and grace. She took us to soaring heights and down to the nitty-gritty of true learning. On the first day of class, Mrs. Springer asked each one of us to stand and give our complete names. By the time it was my turn (she had us go alphabetically so the R's came near the end of the introductions), I'd become very much aware, at the tender age of six, that I was noticeably different. Each one of my classmates had three names - a first, middle and last name. When it was my turn to stand and introduce myself, I had only two names to say - Judith Rinker (came out *Winker*, since I could not pronounce my R's). I was doubly devastated - no middle name and wrong pronunciation of the letter R! I barely held it together through the rest of the day. When Dad picked me up on the motorcycle, I cried all the way home.

An Awful Error Corrected

Upon arriving home, I ran into the house and blurted out in a trail of tears that everyone in the class had a middle name except me. "Why have I not been given a middle name? Woo-hoo, Woo-hoo!" I cried. Mother quickly solved the whole dilemma by sitting me down and saying very quietly, "Well, Judith, we didn't give you a middle name so that you could choose your own." I was floored! *I would get to choose my own middle name!!!* Needless to say, I was ecstatic!

The First Grade Gets Better

The next day I asked to stand and introduce myself again. I proudly announced, "I am Judith Anne (with an e) Winker." Now, I was not noticeably different but *noticeably special*, since I had been privileged enough to choose my own middle name!

Aside: OK, so maybe at this point I didn't quite understand how I mispronounced the letter R. I was in my late 50s before this issue corrected itself - I guess through sheer practice.

Judy Winker With An "R"

For years I was Judith Anne (with an e) (W)Rinker - then I went to Judith A. (W)Rinker - then Judy Anne (W)Rinker - then Judy A. (W)Rinker - and finally to just Judy Rinker. My three initials *JAR* spell the word jar and someone told me, somewhere along the way, that if your initials spell a word you'll be rich. I chose to believe it! Thus, *Skipping Between The Raindrops* has been written by JARinker!!

The Swing

I'll never forget **the moment** Mrs. Springer read the poem "The Swing" out loud to us in class. She was standing in front of a whole wall of windows that showcased the magnificent Western Kansas sky - fluffy white cumulus clouds drifting in a sea of brilliant blue - more spectacular over the prairie than anywhere else in the world. I felt myself soaring away.

> **The Swing**
> *By Robert Louis Stevenson*
>
> *How do you like to go up in a swing*
> *Up in the air so blue?*
> *Oh, I do think it's the pleasantest thing*
> *Ever a child can do!*
> *Up in the air and over the wall,*
> *Till I can see so wide,*
> *Rivers and trees and cattle and all*
> *Over the countryside -*
>
> *Till I look down on the garden green,*
> *Down on the roof so brown -*
> *Up in the air I go flying again,*
> *Up in the air and down!*

This poem was the reason I loved to swing so much. We had an exceptional swing and teeter-totter set behind the house and I spent many exhilarating moments swinging. While soaring through the air so high, I dreamt of becoming a chef, a flyer, a lawyer, a teacher or a writer and fantasized about all the exhilarating travel adventures I would have exploring the world.

Mrs. Springer Returns

Years later, in the 1970's, I tracked down Mrs. Springer's mailing address. I wrote asking her if she remembered me and would she share with me memories she recalled from her teaching days in WaKeeney. In 1978, I received a letter addressed to Judith Rinker. I was so impressed with her response of a six page hand-printed letter on ruled notebook paper that I have included an edited version here:

Dear Judy,

Well, well, well – a letter from that little girl who sat in the second row from the window side of the room and about the fifth or sixth seat back. I can just see that hand going up – eager to tell me about her middle name! I can see in my mind's eye where many others sat and it makes me wish I were back there teaching another group!

So you intend to write about your school days! Well please get busy so I'll be here to read it.

As to remembering incidents after 33 years, please remember that I am also 93 years old. I left WaKeeney at the end of the 1944-1945 year. I'll do my best to think of something.

Ghost and Goblins on Parade

    I do remember that we dressed up for Halloween every year and not only paraded in other rooms but with the whole grade school we led a parade downtown! I guess the teachers enjoyed it almost as much as the youngsters.

    Here is something not quite so pleasant. One little girl ran too close to the swings and had her nose broken. One little boy came to school one day with a very bad cold and of course a really bad runny nose but no hanky. I said, "Why don't you go down to the boys room and take a lot of paper and blow and blow and blow – and stay as long as you like." Well, I didn't see him again that day! I made inquiries and found that someone had told him to go home.

One Christmas we made silhouette pictures of the pupils for gifts to their mothers – I drew from their shadows their heads, and each child cut his or her head out and pasted it on the mounting – black on white or vice versa. Then we put them on the wall above the blackboard until Christmas when down they came to take home. That was a real job and I didn't try it but once.

I had a little redheaded boy named Disney. He said that Walt Disney was his uncle and I believe it was true.

Aside: It could certainly have been true because Walt Disney grew up in Ellis, Kansas, just 15 miles east of WaKeeney.

One morning a little boy was tardy and came running up to me and kissed me and said, "I guess I'm late." All I could say was "Oh well, it won't happen again, will it?"

Oh yes, the three school board members Mr. Hille, Mr. Hutchinson and Mr. Rowley came to visit us. I was surprised but delighted. They stayed a long time and afterwards said that it was because they were enjoying the experience so much. I told them they should come more often.

Then there was a dear little colored girl who lived with her grandparents at the hotel where they did the cooking. She invited us to come to the hotel on her birthday and have ice cream. We did and when we marched through the lobby, each received an ice cream cone and a cookie. We had a grand time and I thanked that little girl so much. She was so proud!

We used to act out stories and one time did "The Three Billy Goats Gruff". We made a bridge with the little red chairs. It happened that one chair slipped and one boy fell into the stream. He scrambled up so fast that it made everyone laugh but he was safe.

I wish I'd kept a diary of my days there – of course, there were things which upset me but I just don't think about them anymore.

Here's something strange. As I write this, I keep feeling that I'm writing to your mother and just forget that it is to one of my pupils. I have to gather my wits and tell myself who you are!

And now I may not have written anything which will help you – you may have a very different meaning of incidents – I don't know. Anyway we have corresponded and I have enjoyed that. Good luck – you have made a good start so keep up the good work.

The best to you!
Bessie F. Springer
Excuse me for not writing this all over – just jump over the errors.

P.S. You might have a paragraph about salaries in those days $125 per month and no asking for a raise. Ha!

Aside: *Unfortunately, it's too late for Mrs. Springer to read my memoirs; perhaps she will enjoy them in heaven.*

Rules To Live By

The Roly-Poly Tomboy

There is certainly no denying that I was a roly-poly kid. Although now, years later looking at pictures from school days with my classmates, I don't look as roly-poly as others thought I did at the time. Needless to say, I took a great deal of razzing as a result of this "perception". Being a "fatty" and a "tomboy" and seldom wearing a dress, it's a wonder that any of my classmates knew my real name, especially since I had trouble pronouncing it.

Humor And Excellence

I very quickly learned two lessons about life that have helped me to this day. First, I learned to laugh at the name-calling. After all, if I fought everyone who made fun of my lack of height, I would have had to fight many of my classmates. Second, I learned to excel. There's only so much ridiculing others can do to you when you laugh at them and then promptly beat them in a game. When challenged, I would often ask, "Do you want to play me right-handed or left-handed?" That immediately set the challenger on edge and gave me an advantage. I could bat left or right-handed, play table tennis or tennis or Jacks or any number of other activities with either hand - it certainly gave me an advantage very quickly. To this day, people tell me they marvel at my agility (now they don't say in spite of being a little on the heavy side but the thought is there). Most people are not aware that I learned these attributes as a matter of survival. I'm convinced that the lessons learned - laughter and excellence - are what has carried me resiliently through life enabling me to *skip between the raindrops.*

Aside: *The above comment concerning my agile movements was written in my memoir notes of 1974 - after 46 years, I have slowed down a little.*

A Touch Of Philosophy

"Good, better, best. Never let it rest.
Until your good is better and your better is your best."

I learned this saying from basketball star Tim Duncan who said this was drilled into him by his mother. I hadn't heard that exact phrasing when I was growing up, but it expresses my philosophy to a T! However, I have added an addendum:

"It's good enough. Some things can rest on good enough."

Grades 2, 3, And Wonderful 4

Onto Second Grade
Another Amazing Teacher

Mrs. Olsen was my second grade teacher and I remember liking her. She was firm but you could tell she really loved us. She did let us get out of our seats, and I can remember sitting on the floor a lot. We memorized many flashcards and learned various sounds and combinations of letters. *Phonics - we knew them.*

Third Grade - *Not My Favorite*

My third grade teacher, Mrs. Files had a diamond ring stolen from her desk drawer. I never did know why it was not on her finger, and I'm not sure its disappearance was ever explained very satisfactorily. I do remember that she got it back but don't think the culprit who took it was ever apprehended. I suspect it was a prank gone bad. She did make this rather nice comment in my autograph book:

> Dear Judith,
> Build castles in the air and put foundations under them. I hope you have success and happiness in life. You have been a very good student this year.
> Sincerely,
> Nina Files

One Of My Favorite Teachers Appears In Fourth Grade

Next to Bessie Springer, my favorite teacher in grade school was Kathryn Billings in the fourth grade. A short, sort of roly-poly person with glasses and a never-ending sense of humor, Miss Billings had the knack of making each one of us want to learn. She was actually a stern disciplinarian, but she made it quite clear that she loved each one of us and that she cared enough for us that we should do our very best at all times.

Dispute - Never Solved Or Always Stubborn

We did, however have a never-ending battle concerning the multiplication tables. I never received a perfect score on any of my math tests as I insisted that $9 \times 0 = 9$ as did $0 \times 9 = 9$. Miss Billings would carefully explain to me time and time again that nine zeros added up to zero, and I kept insisting that nine of something would still be nine. It took me years to really believe that a whole lot of zeros added up to a whole lot of nothing! She taught me much about a whole lot of stuff, but she never managed to convince me of the power of zero! Since she was the teacher, however, she always had the last word!

She wrote in my autograph book the following:

Dear Judith,
As you climb the hills the coming years,
May you travel in high and never shift gears,
With plenty of spark and never a knock
And a joy-filling station in every block
Wishing success and happiness always to a very jolly friend.
Sincerely, Kathryn Billings

Music Fills The Air

During fourth grade some of the high school band members came to the grade school and played solos, duets and trios. The cornet playing of Katy who was a junior in high school entranced me, and from then on all I wanted to do was to play the cornet. Our junior high had a choir and an orchestra. We could start playing instruments in the fifth grade and join the orchestra in the sixth grade. The high school only had a band, so all the string instrument players had to change to other instruments or continue on their own. *I always thought that was unusual.*

Finally, I was allowed to start taking lessons on the cornet in the fifth grade. I was elated. Upon becoming a sixth grader, I was able to play in the school orchestra. Of the 90 students in the junior high, around 30 were in the orchestra. I played cornet through junior high, high school and college where I also played French horn.

WaKeeney was always a musical town. In bygone days, an opera hall graced the main street. It was built in 1884 with 400 seats, ornate murals on the ceiling and walls, large brass chandelier and Rochester electric lamps. Tragically it burned down in 1895. In my day there were many musical opportunities: piano lessons, junior high orchestra of 30, high school band of 60, high school chorus of 60, several high school choirs, community band in the summers, community chorus all year round, numerous church choirs and multiple ensembles.

Final Year Of Grade School

Here Comes Fifth Grade

In our small 2,500 person and isolated Western Kansas town, new faces in our classes were something completely out of the ordinary. It happened so seldom that I believe most of my classmates, to this day, could account for all the "newcomers" we had during grade school.

Jathon

One such newcomer appeared in our classroom on the first day of the beginning of our fifth grade year. I shall never forget when this new boy in our midst was asked by our teacher, Mrs. Clark, to stand and introduce himself to the class. He stood up eagerly as his beautiful blonde hair waved over his handsome face and proudly announced that he was "Jathon, call me Thandy Ott". Through the years we often laughed at his speech impediment as he was unable to pronounce the letter S, but fortunately he had assumed the same attitude as I had about being height deprived - he just laughed. I can't remember a time when he ever let it bother him. *Incidentally, his real name was Jason Ott but he wanted to be called Sandy.* He was a gung-ho person with enthusiastic, different and daring ideas, and for a small school he was a welcome breath of fresh air. It was "Jathon, call me Thandy Ott", who added much variety and spice to each of our lives (more on Jason later).

Integrated?

There were two black students or Negroes, as they were called in those days, in the whole school system. Herschel attended grade school for a short time - a very shy, nice looking boy who didn't say much but whom everyone liked.

Geraldine or Jerry spent the whole time with us. She was a great gal and one whom everyone liked. I treated her like I treated everyone else - with good spirits and a friendly attitude. Her tidbit of wisdom in my high school yearbook the year I graduated reads:

Dear Judy,
I can't think of any verse, but I would like you to know that school won't be the same without you. I thank you for always being so nice to me. I wish you all happiness which I know you will find because you make others happy to have a friend like you.
Your school mate,
Jerry

Were We Or Weren't We?

When I skipped the seventh grade, Jerry and I were no longer so close, but in looking back I do think there might be regrets on all sides. She must have been a lonely girl although she was popular at school, but I'm not sure it occurred to any of us to include her socially in events outside of school. I don't think it was a conscious decision on our parts - we just didn't think about it at all. I believe that had we thought about it, we wouldn't have had any second thoughts at all about including her as she was one swell girl. There were, after all, many of my classmates who didn't participate in outside social events, but they were all great people. Maybe, or maybe not, race was an unnamed barrier - I am not sure I'll ever know.

Judith Is Wished Well

Mrs. Evelyn Clark was my fifth grade teacher and wrote in my autograph book:

Dear Judith,
We have once again reached the end of another year. I hope you enjoyed the year as much as I have. May the future always bring happiness and success to you.

Sincerely,
Evelyn Clark

No Grade School Extracurricular Activities

There were no "clubs" in grade school. We went from 9:00 am to 4:00 pm with an hour for lunch. After school, in other localities there were piano lessons, Girl Scouts, Boy Scouts and church activities. There was a roller skating rink in the municipal hall for a few years which was opened several nights a week.

Meandering Home

Rinker School And Walking Home From City School

The *Rinker School* (a one-room schoolhouse) located on Rinker land was one mile west of our house and four miles east of WaKeeney. It was one of many country schools in Trego County. I asked Mom often why we didn't go there; she never gave me what I considered an acceptable answer. My guess was that since she had attended a similar school, she thought I would get a better education from a city school. It was probably an incorrect assumption since the students who came into high school from the country schools were as intelligent as any one of us "townies". As a matter of fact, the high school valedictorian was a country school boy as were half of the honor students.

On one of our hikes from town to home, Gene and I stopped by the *Rinker School* and discovered a way to enter. It was the only time I ever saw the interior. Years later, when all the country schools closed, it was torn down and the acreage was returned to the Rinkers.

Hide And Seek In The Wheat Fields

Gene was 3 1/2 years older than I and we each led our own lives at school, yet we did enjoy each other's company. Many a time, we did things together and I remember incidents when he would stand up for me which I certainly appreciated. Once in a while when it was a beautiful day, Gene and I would walk home from school sometimes with a friend who lived in our area. The walk from grade school to our house was almost 5 miles. We enjoyed these care-free afternoons darting in and out of the wheat fields, playing hide and seek and yelling back-and-forth to each other.

Our county had no school buses, so in grade school, if parents in the country wanted their children to go to city school they had to take their children back and forth. In addition, something that I recently learned was that the families had to pay tuition of approximately $84 a year per student. In high school, in lieu of buses, mileage was paid from the school district to the parents.

School Happenings

No Trading Here

Since we had no cafeteria in grade school, all the "townies" trekked home for lunch and the country kids sat on the interior concrete steps leading to the gym to eat. We often compared lunches with each other and would sometimes trade. I'll have to admit that I didn't do much trading as Mom fixed delicious lunches. There were always homemade bread sandwiches with butter, ham, cheese, lettuce and mustard (no mayo), or roast beef or wiener spreads, carrots and celery sticks, homemade dill pickles, homemade potato chips, homemade cake or cookies and lemonade or milk. In the winter there would be homemade *chili soup* or vegetable soup.

* *See recipe from the Rinker kitchen at the back of the book!*

Aside: *With lunches like these, who would want to trade?*

Gene And The Tooth Escapade

When the weather was good, after eating inside, we would run outside to play. In the winter, we would run down to the gym floor and play basketball, red rover, tag, dodge ball and any other games which came to mind. There was no lunch supervisor and the office with the only telephone was locked. During one bad winter day we were all on the gym floor playing basketball. The basketball hit my brother in the mouth and knocked his front teeth badly out of whack. There was no help in sight, no supervisor, no phone. I was eight or nine at the time; the only response that came to mind was to run the six blocks to the home of my parents' friends. I ran through the rain and sleet and knocked on their door. Luckily, Minnie was home and I quickly explained the problem. We called my folks to come get Gene. I don't remember how or if I went back to school that day or if my folks picked me up. Gene did lose his front teeth and after this incident, a teacher was always on duty, complete with a key to the office with the telephone.

Playtime

No Organized Physical Education

We had no physical education in grade school or junior high school. Girls had almost no sports opportunities, so you had to be good to play with the boys. Since I was regarded as a tomboy, and it was a label I wore with distinction, it meant that I was good at sports and games and could compete with the guys - Cowboys and Indians, tag, work-up softball and soccer.

The Gang Relaxes

A Good Trait To Inherit

My physical skills for sports were inherited from Mom and Dad who were both well-coordinated. And it certainly helped to have an older brother who was very athletic. However, you did have to prove yourself or you would be left out, and I never had any desire to *sit by the side of the road and watch the race of men go by!* I wanted to participate in the thick of things.

My Friends - Not Too Coordinated

Although many of the guys in my class were well coordinated and eventually a good number of them were on the high school sports teams, most of my girlfriends were not so blessed. I remember many of them being rather spastic. Unfortunately, they were probably not unique. There was one gal, however, who was probably my equal. Everyone knew it was going to be a furious battle when Evelyn and I were on competing teams - as we often were - otherwise the other team wouldn't have had a chance. This "friendly" competition carried all through our high school days, and we remained friends throughout our lives.

Playtime Was A Free-For-All

Playground equipment was probably average for the time. On the side of the school, we had a slippery slide, which for some unknown reason, I had an abject fear of. In fact, the first time I ever slid down one was at the amusement park Six Flags Over Texas in Dallas when I was in my 30s. After being browbeaten into trying it, I went flying down in fear of my life! Two years later, I slid down a super long slide in a salt mine in the Austrian Alps. I loved it! Now I look back with no small regret at all *the slides* I missed in my life which might prove the adage: *You regret not doing things much more than you regret doing them.*

We also had a merry-go-round, teeter-totter and swings. The swings were my favorite. The teeter-totter was not popular with me (probably because I outweighed most of my classmates). The remaining equipment consisted of a semi-high bar over our one and only paved area (the sidewalk in front of the school). Many somersaults were turned on the semi-high bar, and the children's ditty "I see London, I see France, I see _____ underpants" was heard quite frequently. To this day, I have never turned a somersault - even when I taught gymnastics, it was not on my list of things to demonstrate.

Organized Chaos

I also remember playing kick-the-can, Red Rover-Red Rover, London Bridge is Falling Down, Mumbly-peg (played with our pocket knives), lots of Jacks (played on the sidewalk) and marbles (played in the dirt alongside the sidewalk). Of course, our knuckles were rubbed raw either by the concrete or the sandy dirt.

A Field Of Dreams

The sports field was located behind the school and was a large expanse with nothing but dirt. That's where the soccer, softball, Cowboys and Indians, tag and whatever other games we could concoct were played. Having no official equipment, we just put up a couple of chairs for goals or bases and away we went!

Someone would come up with a softball and a bat; I don't think we had gloves. Captains were chosen by volunteering, acclamation or vote. Then sides were chosen by the two captains. One captain tossed a bat to the other; wherever it was caught, the captains took turns placing hand over hand, and the last one on top of the bat would get to choose the first player. The game would commence when every person was chosen. Almost all team games (including Cowboys and Indians) were decided using this "bat" method.

Work-Up Softball

If there weren't enough players to form two softball teams, we played "Work-up". The general set-up on our playground began with players choosing a starting position: 3 batters, 1 pitcher, 1 catcher, 1-3 infielders and 1-3 outfielders. Players would work their way up to the batter position. The batter would bat until striking out or be put out on a base or be put out on a caught fly ball. Then, everyone would rotate to a different position. The "out" batter would go to right field. The right fielder would move to center or left field, that fielder would move to third base and on around - first to pitcher, pitcher to catcher and catcher to batter. The beauty of "Work-up" was that everyone got to play every position as the batter usually didn't last too long, and the game could be played with fewer players!

The Most Popular Game in School – Marbles

My memories concerning marbles are vivid. I was very proud of all the marbles I won through our friendly playground competitions. My favorite "shooter" was a medium-sized dark blue marble with yellow, red and bright blue stripes running around it. It won me many competitions and thus was appropriately named "Lucky". There are four games I remember playing: *Ringer, Lagging, Poison and Fish.*

Ringer

One of the more difficult games, *Ringer*, involved drawing a circle in the dirt/sand of about three or four feet in diameter and then drawing a line across the middle of the circle. Each of us placed several marbles along the center line. The object was to line up at the outside circle and hit a marble out of the circle with your shooter. It was not easy to do and no fudging was allowed.

Lagging

A second game, *Lagging*, was to draw a line 10 to 20 feet away and then see who could get closest to the line. I also think we used this game to see who went first in other games. It was called "lagging" or "Do you want to lag to see who goes first?"

Poison

Poison, one of my two favorite games was played by digging holes in three of the corners of a 10 foot square. Each player tried to shoot his marble around the course, sinking it in each hole. When a marble got back "home," it was "poison" and could "kill" other marbles. Killed marbles belonged to the player who killed them.

Fish

Another favorite game was called *Fish*. We drew the shape of a fish on the ground - usually with one of our fingers or a knife (many of us carried pocket knives for just such an occasion). The fish was about 12 to 15 inches long and 6 to 8 inches wide and a certain number of marbles from each player would go inside the fish. Then we would take turns popping the marbles out. I can remember receiving some marbles at Christmas. Immediately upon opening the package, I set up a *Fish* game using the design in my Mom's carpet on the living room floor.

For Keeps

We didn't have to play "for keeps" but we usually did. Playing "for keeps" meant that you got to keep all the marbles you won during a game. "Lucky" won me lots of marbles.

I Still Have All My Marbles (mostly) Youngsters Don't Have A Clue

Years later I tried teaching marbles at a youth camp. I eventually had to give up, as the skills were so alien to the campers, it was impossible for them to master the techniques with any degree of finesse. I also tried to teach marbles to the students in one of my University recreation classes. Even that was a stretch too far. Perhaps my "unluckiness" in teaching marbles to those of any age had to do with the loss of my favorite shooter "Lucky". I have searched high and low for it through the years but to no avail. Unluckily, "Lucky" has been lost.

Another Failure

My childhood friend and neighbor LaQuita remembers all of our school-day marble playing on the playground. She tried to teach her granddaughter how to play, but she also gave up because her granddaughter just couldn't seem to get the hang of it.

The End Of Grade School

Beginning A New Chapter

The end of fifth grade meant the closing of one chapter in my life. In the fall of 1945, I would skip up the stairs of the red brick building to begin a new chapter into the unknown world of junior high school.

Part III

My Junior High School Promotion

Onward And Upward

In junior high, grades sixth to eighth, I began the real adventure into "growing up". Instead of one main teacher for most of my subjects, I went from classroom to classroom and had "specialists". It was new, exciting and challenging to stay on one's toes with all the different personalities of each teacher.

We Were Musical

One of our "special" teachers throughout grade school and junior high was Mrs. Carter, our music and dance teacher. Although we often acted up during music class, we really did like and respect her. I can still remember learning and singing "America," "Oh Susanna," "My Grandfather's Clock" and hundreds more. We were taught the Virginia Reel, Red River Jig, Pop Goes the Weasel and many more dances which initiated the usual shuffling around of not wanting (*or wanting*) to touch this or that particular boy. It was all great fun and Mrs. Carter stuck with us until we learned and could sing all the musical notes of all the songs and dance all the steps to the jigs and reels.

In the sixth grade we got to join the orchestra! I loved playing the cornet along with all the other "musicians" as we "made lovely music together".

My Favorite Song

One of my all-time favorite songs was Hoagy Carmichael's "Lazy Bones":

Lazybones, sleepin' in the sun....
how you 'spect to get your day's work done?

Never get your day's work done....
sleepin' in the noonday sun

Lazybones, layin' in the shade....
how you gonna get your cornmeal made?

You can't get no cornmeal made....
sleepin' in that evening shade

When taters need sprayin', I bet you keep prayin'....the worms fall off of the vine

And when you go fishin' I bet you keep wishin' them fish don't grab your line

Lazybones, loafin' all the day...
.how you 'spect to make a dime that way?

*You won't make no dime that way....
loafin' in the shade all day*

In my autograph book in May 1946 (sixth grade) Mrs. Carter wrote:

*Dear Judy,
I've enjoyed very much being your music teacher. You have a very nice start on your instrument. <u>Keep working</u>. Lots of success and happiness.
Sincerely,
Mrs. Carter*

Never A Hurdle

Mrs. Acheson who was a tall, gangly lady was one of our junior high teachers, and she rather scared most of us. She wrote in my autograph book:

Dear Judy,

(Aside: *At last, two teachers who called me Judy. I always hated the name of Judith, until I found out it meant "She who would be praised" in Hebrew. I decided that sounded rather nice.)*

Mrs. Acheson continued:

Well, here we are on the last mile – and almost the last hour – everything is in an uproar... here's wishing you the best of luck and happiness.

Lovingly, Mrs. Acheson

P.S. And remember our hike and hurdles...someday perhaps you and I will be able to jump!

Aside: *I have no recollection of this hike, but I do know that I have never learned to jump hurdles and to the present day I have never ever even cleared one.*

Dream Big

In the sixth grade we had a full-time substitute teacher by the name of Bertie Deines. She and her husband (a lawyer in town) were good friends of my parents. I can remember her reading out loud to us from great books of literature and talking to me personally about how great I could be and how much I could make of my life. She truly inspired me to "dream" great things. It would be interesting to know, but I never thought to ask my classmates at the time, if she also inspired them to dream great dreams. Sadly, she died a painful death a few years later when she succumbed to cancer.

The Principal - The Leader

Mr. Noel, the principal, was a huge man and probably seemed doubly large to his grade school and junior high school pupils. Our town had no such thing as a superintendent; the grade school principal was a law unto himself, and Mr. Noel ruled with an iron hand. The same could be said for the high school principal.

Power Play

I'll never forget the day we were all sitting in the sixth grade social studies class. Out of the clear blue, Mr. Noel marched into the room through the open door, walked straight down the first aisle, stopped at the middle desk where Victor sat, reached out his huge hand over the middle of Victor's head, grabbed a huge wad of hair and literally shook him until his teeth rattled. Then, he turned and marched out of the room leaving each one of us almost as shook up as dear Victor.

Alas, I can't remember Victor's indiscretion - probably talking when he shouldn't have been, but suffice it to say, that the lesson being taught was adhered to by each of us even more carefully than before. And I can't remember Victor ever acting up again!

We Were Nice

Children have been known to be very cruel, but I cannot honestly remember many overt acts of cruelty which I saw or was aware of growing up. I'm not really sure if the acts didn't take place or if I were just oblivious to them. However, there were two incidents that I do remember.

But Not Always

There was a fellow a few years older than we were who would come to the playground. He had the shakes and there was obviously something physically wrong with him beyond his control, but we made fun of him. He must have had a terrible life, but we never stopped to think "What if we were like him?"

Some Never Learn

Since I was known as a tomboy, not too many of the kids cared to tangle with me. However, there was a boy by the name of BT who was four to five years behind me. He was large for his age and he liked to bully some of the smaller students. I threatened to meet him one day after school if I heard of him bullying them again. Evidently he didn't stop, so one day I did meet him after school and remember giving him a few wallops. It was not one of my finer hours, but to my knowledge, he quit his bullying ways.

Afraid To Ask The Colonel

His sister was in my class and we graduated together and still see each other occasionally (she lives in our hometown). BT must have been pretty quiet as to his activities (and mine) as Berniece never said anything to me about the incident. Several years ago in WaKeeney, I ran into him on the street and, lo and behold, he was a Marine Colonel. I was dying to ask him if he remembered "the incident" but I didn't have the nerve. *Probably thought he might send me to Boot Camp!*

A Surprise First Period

At the age of 84, I was asked to complete a questionnaire at a doctor's office. One of the questions was "When did you start your period?" As if I could remember! The nurse looked at the questionnaire and then she looked up at me and said, "Well, we'll just put down age 12; that is when most girls start". The question got me to thinking - *when did I have that momentous occasion?*

I was in the sixth grade and my recollection is that at some point during the morning, I went to the girls' bathroom in the basement. Upon pulling down my underpants, I noticed there was blood on them. I had no idea what was happening as I didn't remember feeling sick. I walked up the two flights of stairs to the second floor and asked the principal, Mr. Noel, if I could use the phone. I don't remember what I said to Mother, but she told me to wait and that Dad would be right there to pick me up. I walked back down one flight of stairs and out to the front pavement where about 10 minutes later my Dad zooms up on his Harley-Davidson motorcycle. I don't remember what I thought at the time, but in looking back I have to laugh about the mode of transportation. Upon arriving home, Mother sat me down, told me *some of the facts of life,* and gave me a sanitary pad to start being a woman. *How little I knew!*

Winker Strikes Again!

The summer after my sixth grade year, I went to Camp Lincoln, a church camp, located in a former German Prisoner of War Detention Center about 100 miles northeast of WaKeeney.

Several carloads of parents drove my friends and me to the camp. It was my first time away from home and I was really excited to meet other young persons who were attending camp from across the state of Kansas. When I arrived at the registration table, a lady asked me what my name was. I proudly responded "Judy Winker". Her response was, "Oh, Judy Winker" and I retorted, "No, it's Judy Winker with an R, R-i-n-k-e-r; Winker". She responded, "Oh, Judy Rinker" and I quite proudly said, "That's wight, Judy Winker".

Skipping The 7th Grade

A Daring Request

One of my most daring acts was when I told Mom I wanted to skip the seventh grade and I was hell-bent on doing so. Mother had no objections, but she told me she was going to have nothing to do with it. It was up to me to ask Mr. Noel for permission. So on the first day of school (the Tuesday after Labor Day), I marched myself into Mr. Noel's office and said, "Mr. Noel, I'd like to go into the eighth grade". I can't remember if he even asked why, but had he done so, I would have told him that I thought I fit into the class better. Although I really did like my "old classmates," I just thought I'd like my "new ones" better. And truth be told, my best friends were in the eighth grade.

Granted!

However, I don't remember that he even asked me for my reasons. He just said, "OK, take your books and join the eighth graders." I was actually surprised and shocked to find it so easy. I walked out of his office and walked past the open door of my former classmates. They were waving to me and shouting out "Here we are. Get in here Judy." I just waved and kept walking - actually a little afraid of what was in store for me.

You're In The Wrong Room

When I walked into the eighth grade class, everyone said, "You're in the wrong room" and "Judy, what are you doing here?" I replied, "I'm an eighth grader now." They were dumbfounded and asked me how I did that. I replied, "I just asked." From then on I was walking in high cotton.

A Smart Move

Looking back at the incident I don't know how I had the nerve to do it and in today's world it probably would not be possible - too many hands in the pot, too many tests to take, too many naysayers. *To this day, I believe it was one of the smartest decisions I ever made.*

I Still Thought 9 x 0 = 9

The only negative I was ever aware of in "losing" the seventh grade was that I lost (and never found) the rudiments of algebra. I believed I was at least average to good in math up to that point, except when it came to multiplying by zero. But from the eighth grade on, I barely made it through algebra, geometry and college chemistry. It was all the more amazing that my math skills were so bad since math was among my brother's strongest subjects.

Aside: *Actually, I still see no reason for suffering through any higher math courses.*

New Friends

In-Be-Tweener

I always enjoyed my "old" classmates, most of whom I started with in the first grade, but when I skipped from sixth to eighth grade, I enjoyed my "new" classmates even more. It was a better fit - just like an old glove. It could have been because I was an in-be-tweener. At that time in Kansas, your birthday had to be before September 1 to start the first grade. I was six years and seven months old when I started school. Hence, I was an in-be-tweener.

The Gang

There was a group of us who bummed around together from grades one to six, but "our gang" really came to life when I joined the eighth graders. There were five or six of us who were all friends from being members of the Presbyterian Church. My longest and dearest friendship was with a gal named Peg, a fellow Presbyterian. We shared many adventures during those wonderful and cherished years from the eighth to the twelfth grades. Until recently, we could sit up all night telling and retelling all the dumb, funny, stupid adventures we had, both with each other and with the rest of the gang - which was always fluid.

The Gang

High Jinks On The Farm

Peg and I remember with great clarity one of the many times Peg stayed all night at the farm. We started our evening adventures with a moonlight bicycle ride out on our unpaved, rutted and lonely country road and ended up peeking into our living room windows and scaring my folks half to death.

(They didn't know we were outside the house.) We began scratching on the screens which brought them out of their chairs and charging outside to see who the marauders were. Needless to say, we were sent upstairs without our evening ice cream snack which was a cruel punishment indeed!

My Pal Peg

More High Jinks

While lying in bed, a bit later, Peg looked out the window and whispered to me, "Someone is out by the light tower...really." I gingerly peeked out but could see no one. Peg looked again and began to describe in graphic detail what she was seeing. I looked again, and although I could see no one, the more scared I became. I was just about to bury my head under the covers when Peg broke out laughing for all get-out. She had been pulling my leg the whole time and I fell for it, hook, line and sinker!

Share Your Joys – Well, Sometimes

A note in my diary on February 1947 (eighth grade): *Tonight I have made a motto: Share your joys.*

Then I added: *Sometimes, but not always.*

The Big Baseball Game

One of my most vivid memories was of an evening when Gene took me to town on Dad's Harley-Davidson. It was a big dude and I always loved riding it with Gene or Dad, but I also always felt in fear for my life! We were headed to the high school baseball field where Gene was playing with a group of his friends. We went careening up to the field which was actually on the grounds where the Trego County Free Fair was held each August.

Gene and the Harley

In My Glory

I was in my glory - being in grade school - here with my big brother. At some point during the game, someone said, "Why not let Judy bat?" I was ecstatic! The pitcher threw the ball (probably as hard as possible and thinking *I'll quickly dispose of that Rinker tomboy*), and then I felt the bat connect with the ball for a good solid hit, and I was on my way flying to first. I subsequently scored a run, and I'll never forget Gene's pride in me when he told my parents about the game. *It was a sweet taste of success at its very finest!*

Boxing Comes To Life

Girl Scouts always struck me as a sissy organization, although I eventually became a Girl Scout leader during my school teaching days. I joined up in grade school so I could be with all my friends. We met at the Boy Scout house, as in those days there were certainly no meeting places designated for girls! The one meeting that stands out in my mind was when a friend and I discovered some boxing gloves in the closet. Kathleen and I challenged each other to a sparring match. Both of us started hitting each other rather

Boxing buddy Kathleen on right and friend on left

tentatively, but as time progressed, we began hitting harder and harder. As one of us hit hard, the other would try to hit even harder. By the time it was all over, Kathleen had a bloody nose, and I had a swollen face as well as a very unsure knowledge of whether or not I liked boxing.

New Food - Not So Much

At one point in time, there was a brief attempt to have a "school cafeteria" which was located in an old house several blocks from the school. Although my memories are rather vague about it, anyone who wanted to eat there had to walk. Rain or shine we hoofed it to the cafeteria. I can't remember any of the food except for the day that dumplings were served. Having never had dumplings before, I was unprepared for their taste and was not impressed at all. To this day, I maintain a negative attitude toward the very mention of dumplings. The main problem was that I enjoyed Mom's scrumptious lunches with homemade *cookies* more than any other food.

See recipe from the Rinker kitchen at the back of the book!

Who Made This?

One winter's eve, I was invited to spend the night with a classmate friend of mine. It was always fun to stay all night in town so I welcomed the opportunity. Her Dad was one of the local doctors, and her Mom was active in social events so they were both gone during the early part of the evening. Sue asked me if I were ready to eat and I said, "Sure". Shortly thereafter, we sat down to crackers and a strange looking bowl of soup. I had never seen anything like this, and I asked

Sue what it was. "Vegetable soup," she casually stated. My return question was "Who made it?" Her response, "Well, I don't know. It just came out of a can." I was amazed as I didn't realize there was such a thing as canned soup. Truth be told, my Mom's *vegetable soup* was a hundred times better.

* *See recipe from the Rinker kitchen at the back of the book!*

Aside: *Must say, that to this day I don't go out of my way to have any canned soup!*

My 8th Grade Shenanigans

Sew, A Needle Pulling Thread

I was to come into direct conflict with Miss Gladys McCrae, the art and sewing instructor. It could have had a lot to do with the subject matter as I was definitely not, have never been and will never be, a seamstress. Threading a needle was and is pure torture. (Another story about sewing will be found later.)

Grandmother to the Rescue

Raveling

One of my "big projects" in Home Economics was to ravel a card table cloth and four napkins. I still have the set today as a reminder of the torture I went through in that junior high sewing class. My "other biggie" was a lightweight bed jacket which I conned my Grandmother into doing for me as she was a very skilled seamstress. I've often wondered what Miss McCrae thought of that project! I can only remember Grandmother coming to visit a few times, but fortunately for me, she arrived at the right times when it came to my sewing projects.

Uproar

The Home Economics class was often in a continual uproar as we would get up and move around, talk, laugh and, in general, try to do anything to relieve the dullness of sewing in any way possible.

I'll Stare You Down Any Time

One day the noise obviously got to Miss McCrae and she told us to "shut up". A sudden hush fell over the class as we all took to sewing ever so industriously. Little old me couldn't restrain myself and after several moments of utter silence, I let out a great big, hilarious laugh. Miss McCrae, who was sitting kitty-corner across the table from me, just stared at me, and if looks could have killed, I would have been dead.

And then just by chance, I stared right back at her. The staring went on and on as the room got ever and ever quieter. By this time there were no needles moving - only all "Eyes" on the two of us. After what seemed like an eternity, Miss McCrae dropped her eyes and looked away. I, in turn, lowered my head and began to sew again.

The whole episode probably didn't last more than a minute or two, but it seemed like an eternity at the time. I can't remember an aftermath - except that I still can't stand to sew and still can't thread a needle. *I can, however, outstare my cat and anyone else who feels like challenging me.*

My Sewing On A Kibbutz

The postscript to the above story is that years later when I went to work on an orchard kibbutz in Israel, my first assignment was to the sewing room. I asked someone to thread my needle and to make the thread very, very long! An hour or two later, someone came in and asked if anyone would like to help in the kitchen. My hand went up faster than lightning and I was out of there. I guess the person who made the daily schedule got the hint as I was never assigned to the sewing area again.

Blood Everywhere

I was in the school play during the spring of my eighth grade year. During a noon-time rehearsal I put my right hand on the stage apron and went to leap upon the stage. I slipped and my hand went crashing into a light bulb inside the apron at which point blood began shooting straight up at least a foot!

Someone rushed to get Mr. Noel, the principal (at least one teacher was on noon duty - since my brother's tooth escapade several years earlier), and he promptly revved up his little orange Volkswagen Beetle and away we dashed to the local doctor's office. I can still remember apologizing profusely to Mr. Noel for all the blood that was getting all over his car. Luckily, the only injury to my hand was to an artery which did take several stitches and several months to heal. I still have those scars in the middle of the palm on my right hand.

Side Effect

The accident did have a side effect. Nothing was going to stop me from playing tennis, so I switched to my left hand. I'm still somewhat ambidextrous, as I had to write left-handed for several months also. At the junior high commencement, I received my diploma with my right hand swathed in a bandage, but I had to shake everyone's hand with my left hand.

Pre-Camp Adventure

After I graduated from eighth grade, I spent another week at Camp Lincoln, which I had attended the prior summer. However, getting there proved to be a bit of a challenge. The night before I was to go to town to meet my ride, it rained cats and dogs. The next day, our road was impassable due to all the mud, yet I was determined not to miss this grand adventure. Dad strapped my suitcase over Tarzan, helped me up (no saddle), slapped Tarzan on the rear and off I went across the fields and pastures one and a half miles south to Highway 40. I hoped my ride with fellow campers would be waiting for me alongside the road. Fortunately, Tarzan chose to behave himself and I remained mounted and arrived in one piece. And sure enough, there was my ride. They helped me off Tarzan, unstrapped my suitcase, gave Tarzan an encouraging pat on the rump and off he trotted toward home.

Camp Lincoln

Camp Lincoln was a former Prisoner of War Camp during the years 1943-1945. The accommodations had not improved since the previous summer when I attended, so the camp was still very primitive. There were two large barracks (one for girls and one for boys), a mess hall, a chapel, non-flush toilets and a shower house and playgrounds. But since we were with our "Presby" friends from all over the state, we really didn't care about the "primitiveness" of the camp. We just enjoyed the fun, fellowship and friendship.

One of our favorite activities was travelling on a flat-bed trailer to go to the swimming pool in the nearest town. As we drove through downtown, feet hanging over the sides, we would sing at the top of our voices:

We are the Presbyterian kids,
That name is our name too.
Whenever we go out
The people always shout,
There go the Presbyterian kids.
Tra-la-la-la-la-la-la-la.

Then we would repeat, repeat and repeat. All the folks along main street would smile and wave to us and we would enthusiastically wave back.

Aside: *Dianne also went to Camp Lincoln for three summers 1952-1954. She remembers it as being somewhat primitive as well.*

Holiday Festivities Through The Years

New Year's Eve

I don't remember doing much to celebrate New Year's Eve or Day. We did get to stay up late as we gathered around our trusty radio/phonograph console to hear the ball drop in Times Square and to hear the New Year's Eve celebrations around the country. We also set off some firecrackers in the yard on New Year's Day.

Valentine's Day

On Valentine's Day we gussied up in our red and white finery. The teacher let us have a little Valentine's party where we exchanged mostly humorous Valentine cards and shared our assorted Valentine candies, including candy Sweethearts.

St. Patrick's Day

On St. Patrick's Day, we wore something green to school to escape the tradition of being pinched. According to folklore, you get pinched on St. Patrick's Day for not wearing green because green makes you invisible to leprechauns, and leprechauns like to pinch people.

Easter

The big holiday in the spring was Easter when we dolled up in our new finery, took our Easter baskets with our hand-colored eggs to church and had an Easter Egg Hunt. After church, many of those attending would meet at a local restaurant for Easter Dinner.

Mother's And Father's Day

On Mother's Day we went to church, took Mother out to a local restaurant for dinner and then went home. *I gifted my ironing skills as a present to Mom!* Father's Day was not observed because it was not made an official national holiday until 1972. *Sorry about that Dad!*

Memorial Day

Memorial Day was always a somber time in towns across Kansas; until recently in WaKeeney, high school class reunions were held at the same time. Every five year class, since the founding of Trego Community High School in April 1913, met for individual class reunions on a Saturday, followed by a huge community gala Saturday evening. Sundays were devoted to church and mini-class get-togethers. On Monday, Memorial Day, local high school band members gathered at the City Park and played and marched through town the two miles to the cemetery. A Commemoration ceremony was held in remembrance of fallen veterans and those who have preceded us in death. "Echo taps" were played in tribute to service members who paid the ultimate price. It was always an honor to be chosen to play, and I received the opportunity one year - I was so proud.

After the service at the cemetery, and after flowers were placed on grave sites, many of the "reunioners" would have lunch at local restaurants and then would head home to faraway places. These reunions took place for decades, until no one could be found to organize them, and the gatherings were discontinued - much to my personal chagrin. Thankfully, Memorial Day services at the cemetery have continued.

Fourth Of July

Originally over the Fourth of July weekend, there were harness racing at the fairgrounds and a huge fireworks display in the evening with everyone sitting in the grandstand oohing and aahing! As time went by, the horses disappeared and car racing took their place. For farmers, attending these holiday festivities was typically iffy; if wheat harvesting wasn't finished, work came first!

Trego County Free Fair

The biggest event of the year in Trego County was the Trego County Free Fair. It normally started on Tuesday and ran through Sunday. There were hundreds of displays of local produce, animals and craft projects in the fairground barns. The midway held a carnival with rides of every description and several food booths sponsored by local churches. Throughout much of the day you could hear a barker calling out numbers from the Bingo tent. If you wanted to see a real sight, you could put down money to go into the tent with the World's Tallest Man, the Lady Killer with the Worlds' Longest Beard and on and on. At the grandstand, you could watch the beautiful harness racing and in the evening the jaw-dropping spectacle of all the circus performers.

Part of the Gang at the Fair

I'll never forget the night we watched from a packed grandstand, with everyone holding their breaths, while the high-wire performers put on a daredevil show towering above the crowd. The wind was blowing at hurricane speeds strong enough to bend the high-wire poles as the acts were performed without the benefit of a safety net below. It was truly a stunning, heart-pounding aerial extravaganza!

The week closed out on Sunday evening with a dazzling fireworks display. Everyone looked forward to this wonderful event every summer. And most times, the farmers and ranchers were able to attend as the dates in August were "in-between" field work!

Labor Day

We were usually working over Labor Day weekend, due to all the seasonal field work to be done. School started on the Tuesday after Labor Day, so we always considered Labor Day a day of labor before the freedom of school!

Thanksgiving And Christmas With The Newcomers

All through grade school and into high school, our family took turns having Thanksgiving and Christmas Day festivities at the Newcomers. Alice and Carol had four sons: Ed, Art, Herb, Nelson and one daughter, Nancy. Ed was two years ahead of me; Art was in my high school class; Herb was a year behind and Nelson and Nancy were both younger. The parents sat around and talked while the kids romped around outdoors. It didn't matter how cold it was, we played (seven to eight of us) hide and seek, basketball, softball and anything else we could think of.

Hide Bootsie

One year, we made up our craziest game ever - "hide the pony". They had a pony named Bootsie which we decided to sneak up the inside back stairs to the second floor of their house. The Newcomers' house was large and had jigs and jags in it, so the parents didn't hear us trying to lead Bootsie upstairs. We were all laughing so hard it's a wonder we didn't alarm the household. About half way up, we decided the whole fiasco was not going to be successful, so we clomped Bootsie down backwards and out of the house. And wonder of wonders we did not get caught "in the act". Art and I still laugh about this escapade and many more that we all participated in throughout the years.

The Festive Feasts

Alice and Mother prepared all the food for the "Big Days" and everything was always scrumptious. We had our normal Kansas Thanksgiving and Christmas Day menus - both days consisting of the same traditional fare. There was turkey, mashed potatoes and gravy, bread dressing, cooked carrots, frozen peas and onions, coleslaw, cranberry salad, Parker House rolls with honey butter, mincemeat pies and pumpkin pies. *It was truly a mouth-watering feast.*

Aside: *In my childhood years, I never liked bread dressing, but now one of the joys of living in the south is its cornbread dressing!*

The Joyful Music

After feasting and riotous conversations at the dinner table, the eleven to twelve attendees would all help clean up the demolished delectables and then retire to the piano which both Mother and Alice played. Carol and all his sons had fabulous voices; when added to all the women's voices (especially with Dianne singing soprano and Mom contributing the alto), the Sing-a-longs were loud and lengthy. We would sing for two or three hours with each of us handing more and more music to the pianist to play.

Mom Was Shocked

There was so much fun and excitement packed into a single holiday that on the fifteen-mile trip home in the dark of night I was too tired to ask any questions! This put Mom in a state of shock!!!

Aside: *Each of these holidays was a glorious occasion, and those of us who are still alive, remember all the wonderful moments of our fellowship on Thanksgiving and Christmas Holidays.*

Part IV

Grand Finale
My High School Years

My Exciting Summers

A Full Schedule

During high school, my summers were spent on the tractor plowing with the one-way discs, driving the wheat truck, going to church and music camps, helping with chores and reading. It was an idyllic existence.

Pray For Wind - But Not Too Strong

The fieldwork was unceasingly hot, dusty, dirty and very boring, although I was really never bored. I spent my time day-dreaming, talking to myself and figuring out patterns in the clouds. No place on earth has more beautiful clouds than in the skies of Western Kansas. *I miss those cumulus and cirrus creations, along with the high level immense cumulonimbus clouds, towering to vast altitudes as powerful upward air currents stacked them ever higher and higher above the plains.* Kansas clouds are far more impressive than the lower level cumulus and stratus clouds in central Texas. I could spend hours and hours entranced by the rocking, relaxing rhythm of the tractor going round and round the field. I stared into the clouds and was hypnotized by their endless transformations and fantasized all manner of objects in the sky. It was on just such an occasion that I had a very spectacular "field incident".

Tractor Trance

There I was, engulfed in a beautiful "tractor trance" when all of a sudden, the tractor and I disappeared into a *humongous* hole! The only things above ground level were the tractor's air stack (chimney) and my eyes! I had no idea what had happened; one moment I was driving merrily along enjoying the day and then I wasn't - I was in a giagantic crevasse!!! I quickly turned off the tractor motor, made sure nothing on me was broken (as far as I could tell), and scrambled up the side of the hole by standing on the tractor seat. I was really shaken up but took off across the fields to the house. Upon arriving home, I rather breathlessly told Dad what had happened, and he calmly replied that the hole must have been caused by an oil company that was test drilling for oil years ago. The hole was covered up at some point, but over time a large sinkhole was created. It wasn't there the last time that he had gone over the ground. I don't remember how we got the tractor out but suspect we had to have a winch truck from town. I felt very fortunate that I escaped physical injury, yet my feelings were a tad hurt when Dad did not seem too concerned for *my* welfare.

Aside: *It took a lot to ruffle his feathers. Me, my feathers certainly got ruffled that day!*

Nothing Self-Propelled

Back then, there was no such thing as self-propelled anything. The one-way discs, combines and drills all had to be pulled by tractors. The big caterpillar tractor could pull two or three one-way discs, three drills or two combines. During harvest, Gene would drive the caterpillar tractor; Dad and a hired hand would be on the two combines, and another hired hand and I would drive the two wheat trucks. Later, Dianne would also drive a wheat truck. She would wear her swimsuit while working in the fields, and I think it drove my Dad crazy with embarrassment.

The '37 Chevy Farm Truck (which I still have today)

Pressure-Filled Harvest

I loved driving the 1937 Chevrolet wheat truck. My job during harvest was to drive slowly alongside the tractor until I had the bed of the truck lined up with the wheat chutes on the combines. The combine operator would open the chute and let the wheat churn into the truck bed. Dad didn't want to waste time in stopping to fill the truck, so everything was done in motion. If you went too slow or too fast, the wheat would splash over the cab of the truck and fall onto the ground. Naturally, this was not a good thing. You had to watch the tractor driver as he would be signaling with his hand to speed up or to slow down. After filling the truck (it usually took at least two dumps from the combines), I would hightail it to town, about five miles away depending on which field we were working in, sit in line waiting my turn, dump the wheat, get the ticket and then hightail it back. The objective was to return to the field before the combine bins needed to be emptied into the truck again.

Wind, Wind, Wind

All this time, you were praying for a breeze. Any type of air flow was better than no wind at all, as without the wind the wheat chaff would stick to your sweating skin and itch like crazy. Since there was normally a gale, this wish was usually granted!

The Party Line

One Long And Four Shorts

The phones in the country were all on "party lines" which meant that everyone on your line had a "unique ring". The Rinker ring was one long and four shorts which meant that you had to listen to the phone and ascertain if it was for the Rinkers or for someone else. Eventually, you knew everyone's ring on your line, so if you wanted to listen in on your neighbors' gossip, all you had to do was lift up the receiver and hold your breath. If you were really quiet, they would not know you were on the line - *was I or wasn't I?*

Be Nice To The Operator

To connect to the operator, you just turned the handle on the telephone box. The operator would answer, and you would give her the number you wanted and she would ring it. If you wanted someone on your party line, you rang the number yourself (i.e. one long and two shorts or three shorts and one long), hang up, let it ring and then pick it up and hope that your party was on the line.

Listening In

Our phone was on the dining room wall which meant that everyone in that room, the kitchen and the living room could hear every conversation (at least your side of it). And during our lively meal times, it was almost impossible to take a phone call as we always had great, boisterous conversations with everyone contributing their two cents worth.

My Signal

When I drove the Hudson to pick up friends, I would park in front of their house and honk one long and four shorts, and everyone knew it was me.

Summer Music Camp

Music camp at The University of Kansas in Lawrence, located in the eastern part of the state, was worked into the busy summer schedule.

Too Much Sugar

Two happenings stand out from my music camp days. Whereas Western Kansas was hot and dry, eastern Kansas was hot and humid. The humidity forced me to drink a lot of liquid, mostly sweet tea. After the first week of camp, I decided I could not possibly "intake" all the sugar I was stirring into my tea, so I quit cold turkey. After one week of drinking my ice tea "straight," I have never added another drop of sugar! *This was a step in the right direction to reduce sugar consumption and maintain a healthy lifestyle.*

Too Much Sun

The second happening occurred when I went up to the sun deck of the dorm to sunbathe. Whether I fell asleep or just didn't realize what was happening, I managed to inflict upon myself the worst sunburn of my life. *Not a step in the right direction to maintain a healthy lifestyle!* I lay in bed for several days, because the pain was so severe I couldn't move. *Needless to say, I've been a tad more careful throughout the rest of my life to seek protection from the sun.*

Church Activities

A Choice Of Churches

Most people attended one of the approximately 13 churches in WaKeeney. There were Presbyterian, Methodist, Church of Christ, Christian, Church of God, Pentecostal, Episcopal and Lutheran churches. A Catholic church was established much later, but at this time Catholics had to drive to the nearby towns of Collyer or Ellis for their services.

The Kellisons

Many of my friends were Presbyterians, and we did spend a fair amount of time participating in church life. There were church services and Westminster Fellowship on Sunday, choir practices on Wednesday and various other social gatherings throughout the year. My all-time favorite minister and his wife were LaVerne and John Kellison. They were a breath of fresh air to our congregation. Both truly exemplified what the word "Christian" should mean. They had four children and I have remained friends with the family through the years.

LaVerne Kellison

John Kellison

The Kellison Family

Left to right: Greg, Jan, Steve; sitting: Mark

"You Old Devil You!"

One Sunday morning, a member came who didn't often grace the church doors. After church, as John was shaking people's hands as they left, he looked up and saw Charley. While robustly shaking Charley's hand, he exclaimed, "Why, you old devil you!" Charley, president of the local bank, just roared with laughter.

I Cross The Divide
Trego Community High School

Diary Entry

A diary entry in September 1947 when I was 13 years old:

I am now in high school. I'm just a freshman but I sure am having a lot of fun. For initiation I wore my skirt inside out, my blouse backwards and two different shoes. It was all very uncomfortable.

Pillars of Knowledge

Good Teachers

I probably had no more or no less than my share of good and bad teachers than anyone else. But I do remember many of the ones I had were good and honest people and did their best to help us want to learn.

A Really Decent Human Being

Probably my favorite high school teacher was Wayne Johnston, our speech and drama instructor. He was a powerhouse - dynamic, warm, inspirational and a fantastic teacher as well as being a very decent human being. (*Of course, it didn't hurt that he was really good looking either!*) He was a friend to each of us and yet he brooked no goofing off in his classroom. I have many fond memories of him.

Stuttering No More

One of my classmates, Ross, had a terrible stutter which would have put Mel Tillis to shame. But in Mr. Johnston's speech class, Ross was put at such ease that he would get up, give a speech and never stutter! For someone who didn't talk very much, it was always an outstanding performance.

Not Very Good Cheaters

Mr. Johnston suspected several girls (actually several of my best friends) of cheating on a test. He called them in and confronted them with his suspicions and they all FESSED up. He asked what they thought was a fair punishment, and they settled on dropping their score on the test one letter grade lower. One of my friends took a terrific ribbing when her grade ended up as a D. We couldn't believe that she had only made a C even after cheating and we had quite a few laughs over that.

Happy Journey

In addition to teaching, Mr. Johnston directed the plays we performed; many happy times were spent rehearsing through long evenings of practice on our stage which was on the side of the school gym. Never a leading lady, I enjoyed my second banana parts every bit as much as the leading characters. Six of us took Thornton Wilder's *Happy Journey* to the state competition one year, and I ended up dreaming that I would make my fame and fortune on the stage.

Mr. Johnston quit teaching and eventually worked up to a high position in the insurance business. I have always thought it was a huge loss to the teaching profession.

**Happy Journey Cast – left to right
Judy, Merne, Koly, Evelyn, Howard, & Jason**

In my yearbook Mr. Johnston wrote:

Dear Judy
I'm sure you will always continue to be an aggressive individual with many promising talents. You've been a good student in speech and I think you may have possibilities in radio writing. Don't forget "Happy Journey" and the radio programs.
Wayne (Square it Away) Johnston

Aside: Yes, we used to go to Hays and broadcast the news on live radio.

Mr. Hugh Elliott

Two other teachers I remember fondly were Mr. Elliott and Mrs. Harries. Mr. Elliott was the Vice-Principal, history and Latin teacher. I hated Latin but loved history. I can honestly say that Mr. Elliott was not the most inspiring teacher I ever had. He taught in a monotone and seldom looked up from his desk. We would throw rolled up paper and erasers back and forth across the room, and in his speaking voice he would intone, "Winston Churchill ...would Judy and Howard not throw any more erasers...made all these important decisions." You had to be sharp to catch his reprimand. But he exhibited an intelligence and graciousness, that in spite of ourselves, we learned our lessons.

Mrs. Mary Harries

Mrs. Mary Harries was one of my Mom's best friends (remember, they had been housemates in the teacherage in the 1920's); it was difficult not to call her Mary, which I always did outside of school. She taught typing and was an excellent teacher from whom I really enjoyed learning.

"The Bell Has Rung!"

My most vivid memories of my civics teacher, Paul Nelson, were his opening remarks *every single day of every single class* that I ever had with him. As the bell for class to begin would ring, he would pick up the large round wastebasket in the front of the room. As he walked up and down the aisles with the wastebasket, each of us would deposit our chewing gum in it as he said, "The bell has rung! Let us govern ourselves accordingly."

One day in class Mr. Nelson asked me, "What is air transportation?" I was momentarily stumped as I had no idea what he wanted as an answer. Finally, I decided (*quite smartly* as I remember) that the only credible answer was "transportation by air," which I said with a great deal of firmness. My classmates, quiet until then, erupted with a roar. I can't remember the outcome of the incident, but I've always felt that I probably did not give him the answer he wanted.

Another 7th Hour

A later note in my diary (may or may not have had anything to do with the above incident) stated: *I received seventh hour detention which was that dreaded hour after school in the library, for misbehaving or some such thing from Mr. Nelson. All of us culprits sat in the study hall and twiddled our thumbs while everyone else went home, played sports, or participated in other after school activities.*

What? An A+!

On May 18, 1948 (end of my freshman year) I took a civics test in Mr. Nelson's class. I was the only one who scored 100 and I received an A+. What a surprise! *I wondered if Mr. Nelson was impressed.*

Memories Linger

Twenty-one years later, I was having a Coke with Kathryn, a classmate of mine, in a local WaKeeney drugstore. We were talking and laughing about "old times" (it was she who encouraged me to finish my book which I told her I had started several years before), and when Paul Nelson's name was mentioned, we both, as if a quarter had been put in a jukebox, chimed in with those infamous lines, "The bell has rung! Let us govern ourselves accordingly," and we proceeded to burst out laughing.

Aside: *In retrospect, it's probably pretty sound advice. Mr. Paul Nelson eventually became a school superintendent. I often wondered if he had an opportunity to use those two lines very much in his new position.*

Physical Education?

Not A Priority

Physical education was never considered a priority subject at any time in the WaKeeney school system. We never had any PE in grade school or junior high school; there was a required semester or two in high school and then it could be selected as an elective class. Any time or effort put into the teaching of it was definitely an afterthought.

The Off-Target Girls

She Done Me Wrong

One of the teachers I most enjoyed in high school was Caroline Hamma from whom I took an elective physical education course in my junior year. I shall always hold a slight grievance against Miss Hamma as I received a C grade in archery during one of the six-week grading periods. Since I was one of the two or three really "talented" sports women in high school, I always felt as if she had "done me wrong". It mattered little, to my way of thinking, that my arrows never seemed to find their way to the target!

Miss Hamma wrote in my autograph book the following:

Dear Judy
Stay, stay at home my heart, and rest;
Home-keeping hearts are happiest,

*For those that wander they know not where
Are full of trouble and full of care;
To stay at home is best...*
(**Aside:** I obviously did not take this advice to heart!)
Good luck on your tennis playing - you've got the makings of an outstanding athlete.
*Wish I might be here to see you uphold my predictions.
Caroline Hamma*

Aside: *One does notice, doesn't one, that she never says anything about my archery skills?*

Varsity Sports

The Sport Of Kings (And Queens)

Gene and I were on the high school varsity tennis team together (he was a senior and I was a freshman). I have always thought it strange that in the early 1950's isolated

Western Kansas had a thriving tennis culture. We played singles, doubles and mixed doubles, and I lettered all four years. The tennis team was co-ed and the guys and gals traveled together for the varsity competitions. During my freshman year, I occasionally played mixed doubles with Gene, and I played women's doubles with my favorite partner, Delores, until she graduated. We played big schools and little schools; we even played Dodge City which was a much larger school than ours.

The Double Fault Kid with Friends and Coach

My Life-Long Love For Tennis

The only tennis courts in town were located at the high school. There were three concrete courts. I started playing in the fifth grade, continued playing through high school, and later taught tennis throughout much of my teaching career. I never had a formal lesson until high school; but since Gene was an avid player, I picked up many tips from him.

Since the courts had lights, I would often play until ten or eleven o'clock, and on the way home in the Hudson, I would meet my Mom coming to town to check on me.

Aside: *No cell phones in those days.*

Girls' Softball Team – Sort Of

We did have a girls' softball team, but there was no league and the games were rather "catch as catch can". *Looking back, I wish my friend Evelyn and I had had enough gumption to ask, "Where are the organized sports for girls?"*

T-Club – Guys Only

The T-Club, named for Trego Community High School, was the sports organization for boys, and the club sponsored many of the school dances. Almost everyone went to the dances and had a good time. The dances were held in our small gym, giving them a rather "intimate" feeling. Varsity boys' basketball games were played in the city auditorium because the school gym was not large enough.

Intramural Activities

Noon-Time Fun

The girls had to be content with our intramural activities which were played mostly at noon. We had tournaments in basketball, table tennis, archery, softball, tennis, volleyball and hand soccer.

Hand Soccer

I have never known who originated the game of hand soccer, but it became one of my all-time favorite sports. I taught it for three years in my first teaching job in junior high and high school in Utah. I've never seen it played anywhere else, and I've never known anyone else who knew anything about it. *I should publish the rules myself someday.* We played it with a volleyball on the gym floor (the basketball court). You hit the volleyball on the floor with your fist, and the object was to get it through a goal (two chairs or whatever) at each end of the gym. Two teams played, with any number of players. It always turned out to be a wild melee – I loved it!

My Best Friend

A Real Wit

My best friend, whom I regard with much love and affection, was an independent, red-headed beauty named Peggy. She had one of the greatest wits I have ever known. She could entertain all the gang for hours with stories and jokes – all complete with motions, giggles and belly laughs. Every story was hilariously funny and some just a little more or less raunchy. Where she learned them all or how she remembered each one with all the nuances was one of her special talents.

My Pals Sharon, Peg and Hanora

The Gal With Freckles

And no one could possibly have had more freckles than Peg. She fessed up ownership of all her freckles when she wrote in my autograph book (sometime between 1944 and 1947) the following:

Dear Judy
I'm not an eastern beauty
I'm not a southern rose
I'm just a Kansas girl
With freckles on my nose.
Love,
Peggy

The Best Scrambled Eggs Ever

I particularly liked staying all night with Peg as there were always stories to tell afterwards. Her Dad, Charles Gibson, was the part-owner and the pharmacist at Gibson's Drug Store (which is still functioning today with an old-fashion soda fountain, pharmacy and gift shop). Nicknamed

"Brick" for his flaming red hair, he snored louder than anyone I have ever heard. His roars blasted throughout the house, and we spent much of the night giggling. However, I really looked forward to the breakfasts. Her Mom, Ruth, made what I consider to be the best scrambled eggs of anyone I've ever known.

***Aside:** Ruth's eggs were soft and moist and melted in your mouth, whereas my Mom usually prepared scrambled eggs dry and crumbly. After many sleepovers, I found I profoundly preferred them soft and moist. When mine come out that way, I think of Peg's Mom. Unfortunately for my taste buds, I think about my Mom far more frequently.*

The Night Prowler

My brother's room was right down the hall from mine separated by a jagged hallway. One night my friend Peg was staying over, and we were just about asleep, when all of a sudden she sat up in bed and said, "Eugene, you get off that floor right now." By that time, I was awake and flicked on the bed light, and sure enough, here comes Gene through my door grinning sheepishly and asking Peg, "How did you know I was here?"

To this day I don't know how Peg knew that Gene was creeping down the hall with the intent to scare the daylights out of us. She was probably just awake enough to hear the floor creak, as it was prone to do when being walked on. I never heard a sound. Peg also says that she does not remember hearing anything - just had a feeling. Actually, I think the most surprised person among the three of us was

Gene who was very disappointed at having his big scare of the night thwarted.

Ghost Piano

One night the folks were in town at a bridge party and were expected home around 11:00 pm. Peg and I were amusing ourselves playing pool in the basement. Trouble, the kitty, was batting a table tennis ball around on the floor. All of a sudden, we both looked at each other and said, "Did you hear that?" We each replied, "Yes, someone is playing the piano!" We thought it might be the cat, but no, Trouble was curled up in the corner fast asleep, exhausted from his scampering around.

In those days no one ever locked their doors, so it could easily have been that someone had entered the house. With our hearts racing, we rushed up the stairs, ran through the hall to the living room and made a beeline to the piano. NO ONE was there. With fear and trepidation we searched the rest of the house but came up empty handed. *To this day Peg and I swear that we heard the piano being played, but this mystery has never been solved.*

Aside: *After November 1959, when the Clutter family murders took place 130 miles south of WaKeeney in Holcomb, Kansas, everyone began locking their doors.*

A No Show

A Special Night On The Town

Eventually, Gene and I learned which floorboards squeaked so we could avoid them in order not to wake the folks and evade punishment when entering the house after "curfew". Creaking floorboards were not the issue one late night. When I was a freshman, I received special permission to go to a midweek movie downtown - a rare treat indeed. Gene was supposed to pick me up after the movie outside the theater. I waited and waited, but Gene was a no-show, so I walked to the local high school hangout. By midnight, still no Gene and I was frantic. I just knew the folks would never let me go out again during the middle of the week. Shortly thereafter, Gene appeared on the scene, proud and self-confident after spending the evening with some friends stealing watermelons. I was furious! Upon arriving home, we quietly climbed the outside stairs to his bedroom to keep from waking the parents at all costs. As I tipped-toed toward the dark hallway to my room, I stumbled over a cluster of marbles Gene had left on the floor and they scattered in every direction. The racket was unbelievably loud! Now, Gene was furious and I was quaking in my boots. But luck was on our side, as the noise failed to awaken our parents from their slumbers. The next morning, when the folks asked us what time we got home, Gene and I just burst out laughing.

Sis Dianne and the Infamous Exterior Stairway to Second Floor Bedrooms and Sleeping Porch

Crazy Escapades

May We? No!

Then there was the time that Sue, Joyce, Peg and I went with my parents to see the boys' basketball team play in the regional playoffs in Hays, 30 miles away. It was a game on a school afternoon, but since Gene was playing, we really wanted to go!

My folks came to pick us up at lunch-time, and after we climbed into the car, Mom asked us if we had received permission to leave the school premises. We had not. Peg and I were elected to run in and ask the principal if we could miss classes. Peg and I entered the principal's office and announced to him, "We are on the way to Hays to go to the tourney with my folks, Sue, and Joyce; that's OK, isn't it?" When he responded, "Well, no, it isn't," we were momentarily stunned and found ourselves at a loss for words until one of us turned to the other and said, "OK, let's go." At which point, we turned on our heels, left the principal with his mouth agape, and ran out to the car. After a short discussion, when we all stated we were willing to take the consequences, the folks decided we could go. None of us were the "playing hooky type," so we didn't think we'd get punished too severely. We did pay for our folly upon our return, as we each got three dreaded seventh-hour detentions (4:00 pm to 5:00 pm), but we all decided it was well worth it.

Birthday Party

In January 1948, I wrote: *Went to Sue's birthday party (and mine). Sure had a lot of fun. Danced most of the time.* (Sue and I both had our birthdays in late January.)

Fun In The Sun

One day a gang of us took off in the Hudson and went out to Tidball's ranch. *I'm sure I couldn't find it today if I had to, but back then it was an adventure.* We took our picnic lunches and as we ate them and drank sodas, it got hotter and hotter, so we decided to take our shirts off to lie and sit in the sun. We couldn't believe our own nerve - lazing about in only our shorts, pedal pushers and bras!

Girls Just Want to Have Fun!

A Beautiful Winter's Day

Ice Skating Party

One Sunday winter afternoon, a whole group of us went ice skating on one of the country ponds southwest of town. It was colder than a well digger's tail, but clear and crackling crisp with the sky as blue as ice. In other words, it was a fabulous day for ice skating.

Have You Ever Heard Of Ice Burning?

Gene and his buddy Teg were spending their time "burning the ice," which is to say they were lighting a match to it. The ice would sizzle and bubble, then leave a little mound where it had been burned. As a result, there were numerous little mounds scattered all around the pond.

Help! I'm Falling!! I'm Taking A Dip!!! I'm Sinking And I Can't Get Out!!!!

It was one such mound that I went skating merrily over, only to disappear almost out of sight, as the damned "ice burning" had weakened the ice to such an extent that my body just sank straight down vertically into the frigid pond water. My head and arms were all that were showing. As the ice continued to crack around me, a life or death situation developed, which needed immediate action.

Human Chain

Gene, Teg and many others laid down flat on the ice, starting at the shoreline, and formed a human head to foot chain. With much careful pulling, tugging and shouting, I squirmed my way up to the edge of the ice and wiggled my way back to shore with a lot of help from my friends. Needless to say, upon hitting dry land I was one frozen block of ice. Memory fails me as to whether or not we told Mom and Dad about the incident. They would have been horrified at the whole scene.

One of my classmates who was present at the incident wrote in my yearbook the following:

Dear Judy,
I hope when you go skating next time the ice is thicker.
Ernie

Odds and Ends

Pinochle Party

In February 1948, I wrote: *I went to Merne's party. We were supposed to dance but we all played pinochle. Ever since then we have played a lot of pinochle. Had my first pinochle party just the other night.*

More Laughter

Our game of choice was pinochle *(none of my classmates played bridge);* many a day and night were spent around a card table playing for all we were worth. Actually, if truth be told, we spent most of our time telling and listening to jokes and stories. Peg and Sharon were the ringleaders in the joke telling; where they ever came up with the hundreds they told was beyond me. Some were risqué (of course), but mostly they were just downright funny. I always thought that Peg could have been a professional humorist as she could imitate accents and mannerisms of others to a T.

The Greatest Game

When my brother went away to college, he joined bridge groups and became an avid duplicate player. Later in life, my sis became a master duplicate player and told me that her two greatest passions in life (other than her husband, John) were playing bridge and reading. I still think it's the world's greatest game, but I did not play much in my adult life until a few years after my retirement when I was asked to join several bridge clubs. Since then, the camaraderie and scintillating strategies of the game have been a major joy.

Proud Parents

The folks would be really proud of all of us as we have used, in different ways, the gaming skills which they carefully taught us. I do play a mean game of poker, several domino games and various other table games, including Ding Bat, *where my inherited bluffing skills come in very handy.*

Aside: *Thanks Dad for my inherited bluffing skills!*

Lorrine's Slumber Party

We were all invited out to Lorrine's house in the country one night for a big slumber party. As everyone well knows, slumber parties are not what they seem as no one ever "slumbers". "Slumber-less" parties would be a more apt description of the shenanigans. Her folks were out-of-town, so the eight or so of us had her home to ourselves – or so we thought.

Around 11:00 pm we began to hear noises outside; first one shutter would bang and then another; then the howling started and then a peck on the window. Needless to say, we were all scared to death. We would run from one side of the house to the other, bolting the doors behind us. At different times, as we moved from one room to another, one of us would venture a peek out the window, but we never saw anything. At one point, there was a terrific banging on the back door, but by that time we were so scared we would not have opened it even if God himself/herself had announced her/his presence.

The next day one of Lorrine's brothers and his friends proudly proclaimed that they had been the culprits, but by that time we were in no mood to do any forgiving, especially since it was so soon after our "sleepless slumber" of the night before.

Ice Storm

Diary entry on March 1948: *We had the worst snowstorm since 1903. It snowed more than 22 inches. Luckily, I got to stay in town with my friend Peg. The next day there was no school and so at 10:00 am I went out and started to scoop the driveway. Before I was done, I practically had the whole neighborhood of kids helping out. There was Jerry, Joyce, Darrell, Janice, Cynthia and me. Cynthia and I finally went and roused Peg out of bed so she wouldn't miss all the fun – although, she did miss most of the work!*

Snowbound Judy and Gene
Dianne Ready for the Snow

How Can This Be?

Mumps Appear

Since I was seldom sick, it was a major event when I did come down with something. On Sunday, April 11, 1948, my diary entry reads: *Guess what? I have the mumps. It sure made me sick! (It ought to.)*

The following day I wrote: *I'm not able to eat very well. It sure does hurt!*

I'm Remembered

The next day Gene brought me home a bundle of letters from school. My reaction then was *"Sure was fun to be sick!"* But on the following day I was sorely disappointed when I received ... nothing. The next day more than made up for my lack of letters the day before, as not only was I the proud receiver of many more letters, but I had two "song requests" played for me over local radio station KXXX (also known as K Triple X) located 80 miles away in Colby. One song played was "Now is the Hour" requested by Jan, Spitz, Sue and Hanora. The other request was "Dance, Ballerina, Dance" from the PE class.

Peeking Into The Prom

On the evening of April 15, I was feeling much better, and I talked Mom into letting me go to town and pick up my friend Sue. We went to peek into the high school gymnasium where the junior/senior prom was taking place. It was a magical sight. Gene, a senior at the time, wasn't there. As a member of the track team, he was at the Kansas University Relays in Lawrence. He returned the next morning with a third-place medal for his efforts on the Medley Relay team. He was the anchor quarter-miler. *I was so proud of him!*

Aside: *You will notice here that there was no girls' track team!*

No Way!

The day after I returned to school from my bout with the mumps, I was scheduled to play in a tennis match. You can imagine my chagrin after having played the first set to be told I couldn't finish the match. Someone had called the doctor who said I wasn't to be playing at all. I was furious.

Adding Insult To My Illness

To add insult to injury, I wasn't allowed to play in a softball game the next day either, although I was allowed to travel with the team to Grainfield where I could root the team on. The following week when I was "officially" cleared, I played catcher the whole game. Incidentally, we did win both contests.

The Smoking Saga Continues

Official Smokers

Sharon and Peg were the only two persons, as far as I know, who officially smoked. That earned them both a reputation of being a little wild. *It didn't take much in those days to be out of the norm.* Sharon could always be counted on for shenanigans of some sort, but always through the entire hullabaloo, she would be her usual caustic, witty self. Tall and beautiful, she lived her life in her own way and was another one who could keep us all laughing. Sharon's Mom was a beautician in town, and several of us had our hair done at her beauty shop for special occasions. We had several slumber parties on her roof and since one-half was flat it made partying a breeze.

More Jokes And Smokes

Another day, our gang of six to eight persons piled into the Hudson for another adventure. Our usual *modus operandi* was to tell jokes, mostly by Peg and Sharon, laugh uproariously and then just smoke Sharon and Peg's cigarettes. The car was often so filled with smoke it was a wonder that the people in the front seat could see the people in the back and vice versa.

We All Contributed

My Friend Darlene, the 2nd Best Cornet Player I Know.

After hearing all the "Can you top this?" jokes from Peg and Sharon, others would get a chance to throw in their jokes. Darlene, a good friend from a country school and a fellow cornet player, was always good for a few laughs. Elaine, Shirley and whoever else was in the Hudson would chime in. It was a wonder that we all didn't become walking joke encyclopedias.

Aside: To this day, I can neither remember jokes, even the ones I really like, or tell them with any aplomb. I was strictly a sounding board and could laugh with the best of them. The one and only joke which I could remember, and still remember to this day, has become outdated and is no longer apropos. Actually, I can't think of a more wholesome way of growing up than doing the fun, innocent, and non-threatening activities and adventures we shared together.

Wiener Roast At The Farm

One afternoon I had a wiener roast at the farm with about eight of the gang. After gorging ourselves, we retired to my room upstairs where we indulged in the never-ending joke and smoke session. Yes, we all lit up.

More Of The Same – Not Yet Busted

Well, it took only about 20 minutes until the smoke began to filter through the air-conditioning ducts throughout the house. It was shortly, very shortly, that Mom called upstairs, "Judy". I went to the top of the stairway, opened up the door and said, "Yes, Mom." "Are you girls smoking up there?" she asked. With a straight face, my body enveloped in smoke, I replied, "Just Peg and Sharon." I could sense everyone in the room rolling with laughter, and whether Mom really believed me or not, it seemed to satisfy her as she did not come upstairs.

When I walked back to my room, it was through a thick fog. Thank goodness for Sharon and Peg as they smoked "in public" and could take the brunt of all our smoking antics. It is a wonder that we didn't burn the house down! We always admired both Peg and Sharon as they had the courage to tell their parents that they smoked; none of the rest of us did.

Aside: Actually, only Peg and Sharon smoked on a daily basis; the rest of us just smoked when we got together.

Throw In A Little Beer Miller?   High Life?

Peg – Our Errand Gal

One of our more daring escapades was when a whole gang of us were in the infamous Hudson, and we persuaded Peg to go into the bar at Trego Center to buy beer. Trego Center, ten miles south of WaKeeney, consisted of a bar and a Lutheran Church. The Lutheran Church is still functioning, but the bar/store has long since fallen by the wayside.

The details of how Peg talked the bartender into selling her the beer are shrouded in mystery, but none of us will ever forget the look of unadulterated impishness on her face as she came bounding out of the bar with a six pack of bottled Miller High Life. We asked her what she said to the bartender, and she replied that she was given a choice between Miller and High Life. She didn't realize that the bartender was "pulling" her leg so she responded, "High Life!" We laughed ourselves silly.

Living the High Life!

Miller? High Life?

I have always liked the sound of the name and whenever I see a Miller High Life or spot anyone drinking one, my mind is invariably flooded with memories of that day. I'll never forget the image of Peg with beer in hand, her red hair streaming, giggling up a storm and dashing to the car as if the coppers were on her heels.

Aside: To preserve my own image, especially since I was driving, I did not then nor have I ever liked beer – not Miller High Life or any other kind. But it was a wonderful day as we spent most of it laughing our heads off.

Making Music

The "In Tune" Cornet Section

Lorrine, Darlene and I sat next to each other in band, each thinking she played the coolest cornet, and each believing that one of our other classmates was the most off-key player ever. He always played as loud as he could, slurred everything and didn't play the right notes half the time. My good friend, Art, also played cornet, but since he was an athlete, he didn't always get to perform with the band.

Music – Very Popular

Out of 200 students in high school there were 60 in the band. We didn't think anything about it, but we had at least 20 from our class of 56 in the band. And at least 8 to 10 of the 20 were from country schools so they were just learning to play their instruments. There were definitely more girls in the band due to many of the guys being on the athletic teams. The highlight of my high school cornet playing came when my parents gave me a new cornet during my junior year.

Aside: *I still have that cornet and I still play it every once-in-a-while.*

The Award Winning Marching Band

Many Musical Groups

We had a marching band, a concert band, a pep band, mixed chorus, girls' chorus, boys' chorus and various ensembles. We liked our band and chorus teachers, of which there were only two during my high school years. Mr. Mitchell was the director of all these music groups for three years. Mr. Kraus took over during my senior year. It is amazing that one person conducted all these musical groups, gave lessons and kept his sanity! I directed the pep band in my senior year, and we played at all the boys' basketball games and pep rallies. *I loved directing the band and I have used my directing skills leading singing throughout my life.*

Fools' Names

For some holiday event or marching band contest, our band went to the neighboring city of Hays. Mom and Dad drove four of us to the event. (We had no school buses so everyone had to get their parents to take them as those of us who had personal cars could not use them for school events.) The four of us went into the Lamer Hotel to go to the bathroom before we started to march. It was the nicest hotel in downtown Hays and near the beginning of the parade route. Like all bathrooms at that time, kids had written their names and silly ditties on the walls of the toilet stalls. We decided we should be famous also, so as we giggled like crazy, we wrote our names with pencil on the walls. We left the bathroom really proud of our work. A few minutes later here comes Mother furious as all get out. **"You girls get in there and erase your names immediately,"** she said with a very stern voice. And then she added, *"Fools' names like fools' faces always appear in public places."* Boy, we headed back into that bathroom as fast as our legs could carry us and erased like crazy.

Aside: I've never forgotten Mom's Words of Wisdom.

My Sis, Dianne

The Musical Equestrian

My sis, Dianne, was six grades behind me so our paths seldom crossed. She, contrary to me, was a great equestrian and also exhibited a higher technical aptitude on the piano than I. She followed me in the musical arena as she played saxophone in the high school band and excelled in piano. She became a fine musician and choral music teacher, giving private piano lessons after her teaching days.

A Lot Of Horses

When quizzing Dianne about her memories "growing up" on the farm, I discovered much about horses! I don't know where I was (probably with my friends in the Hudson smoking and listening to jokes), but I remember little about all the horses that she had. She even thought that Tarzan was Gene's horse, but I think we must have shared him. For two years, the Newcomers loaned Dianne a horse named Bootsie (of the stairway fame). Later Dad bought Dianne a horse named Cricket for $100, at that time a very expensive horse. A couple of months later, Dad inadvertently left Cricket's gate open and the horse got into some spoiled wheat in an adjoining area. That was the end of Cricket. The next horse was a $65 purchase named Shorty; he died Dianne's junior year in high school. Dad *finally splurged* $25 on a horse called Smoky. He was a wonderful horse to ride, but rather wild. A few times Dianne was thrown off when "on top of old Smoky". Dad sold Smoky when Dianne was in college.

Dianne on Top of Old Smoky

Dianne and Smoky - Sandra and Shorty

Best Friend Sandra And Shorty

Shorty was a gentle riding horse which was good since during Sandra's visits she and Dianne usually rode him bareback and double. Dianne would often ride _alone_ back and forth between their homes, a distance of 15 miles. Those two girls loved horses and spent many an hour riding all over the countryside. In the summer of her eighth grade year, Dianne showed Shorty at the Trego County Free Fair. There was no horse trailer or saddle, so she rode bareback all the way to town and won third place which she was really proud of, especially since she had no idea what she was doing!

Remember "Jathon, Call Me Thandy Ott"?

The Eye Opener

During our senior year, Jason and I decided that the school newspaper was much too conservative. It was a mimeographed production and was absent of any "important" information (gossip) which insulted our intelligence, our pride and our eyesight. So, we started our own "off campus" newspaper called *The Eye Opener*. We had an official space in the newspaper office downtown, which published the *Western Kansas World* (still in print today). Our staff wrote the stories, sold the advertising, set the type and distributed *The Eye Opener* at school for ten cents a copy.

It was a really daring venture and it managed to keep us both (as well as many of our friends who contributed their time in writing and advertising skills) out of any serious trouble for the whole year. Plus, we loved doing it.

Judy <u>W</u>inker and <u>Jathon Hot</u> Go to the Prom

Senior Prom Date

And who would have guessed that "Jathon, call me Thandy Ott" would become my date for the senior prom. His folks offered their home for an all-night party for the whole class (56 strong), and we managed to enjoy ourselves clear through to breakfast the next morning. A great time was had by all.

Back To Tennis

A Signature Event

I had been unbeaten in singles tennis all through four years of high school, and one of my major goals was to remain so. We had an important match scheduled the first week of May at our school with a "big time" opponent – Dodge City. The wind was blowing ferociously! At one point the tennis ball bounced on my side of the net and before I could get to it, the wind had already blown it back to my opponent's side of the court. It was a hard-fought match, but eventually I lost! I was devastated!!!

Revenge - Thwarted

The only motivating factor that saw me through the next two weeks was the knowledge that I could redeem myself at our return match with Dodge City the day before graduation. I lived for that day, but disappointment came by way of a torrential rain storm! The match had to be canceled permanently, and I never got to increase my winning record.

Aside: *Of course, it might have gone the other way, and I might have had two losses instead of one! We'll never know!*

Our Exciting Senior Sneak

A Fitting Conclusion

My friendly sports competitor, Evelyn, who was our senior class president (all of our class officers were women), was instrumental in getting permission for our class to go out-of-state for our Senior Class Sneak. As far as I know, we were the only class ever allowed to do so. All of our class members were on the bus which was in front of the hotel where we had gathered to depart. A friend of mine, Jan, looked out the window, jumped up and scurried off the bus as the door was closing. Her boyfriend had come home from military service and was waving to her from the sidewalk. He had just arrived in town, so she was the only person who didn't go on the Senior Sneak with us.

State Pen

Jan, however, did miss all the fun the rest of us had in Colorado Springs. Two particular memories stand out on that trip (in addition to seeing all the many wonderful sights in Colorado Springs). The first unforgettable memory was a tour of the Colorado State Penitentiary. It impressed upon all of us to walk the straight and narrow paths in our future lives.

Walking In And Walking Out

The second happening was when a whole group of us (8 to 10) walked into a rather nice restaurant in downtown Colorado Springs. We were seated at a large round table; our glasses were filled with water and we were handed menus. We each glanced at the menu, and then at the same time we each looked up, our eyes met, menus closed, all rose and walked out of the restaurant! When we reached the sidewalk, we looked at each other and exclaimed, "Wow!" We obviously, at the very exact moment, realized that the restaurant was way beyond our means.

The End Of High School

I MADE IT!

Judy Graduates

My graduation took place in May 1951, and in those days we had both Baccalaureate and Commencement ceremonies. Baccalaureate was a religious service held in our gymnasium, and ministers from various churches in town participated. Several nights later our Commencement was held; here some in the class were honored for special achievements. Inductees into the National Honor Society (I was one) were recognized, and the Valedictorian, Salutatorian and the keynote speaker addressed the graduates. We walked across the stage to receive our diplomas and moved our cap tassels from the right to the left. Although I am sure both these events were auspicious occasions, I have no clear memories of either!

Aside: I imagine that I did breathe a sigh of relief!

Onto The Next Life Adventures

Well, we have come to the end of my sojourn sagas birth through high school. These many decades later, I still feel as if I have been leading a charmed life *Skipping Between The Raindrops*. As I have every intention of living a few more years (actually, a lot), I imagine that there will be many more occasions for **Skipping**.

Epilogue

Catastrophic Events

No, This Can't Be True

During the spring of my senior year in high school, the most catastrophic tragedy of my life "down on the farm" occurred Sunday, March 11, 1951. My brother came home for a weekend visit from the University of Kansas where he was a junior. I was already enrolled at the University of Kansas for the fall of 1951. I would be a freshman and Gene would be a senior.

The weather was turning very bad Sunday morning, so we decided not to go to church, but Gene said he should get an early start for the drive back to Lawrence so he left around 8:30 am. After he left, I went upstairs to my room to read for a while as Mom and Dad were reading in the living room.

Around 11:00 am, someone knocked on the front door. I heard Mom and Dad opening it and greeting two male friends from the Saturday Night Bridge Club. I was on my way down the stairs when I heard my Mom let out a scream. "What's wrong?" I asked, although I already had a premonition about the answer.

In the snow storm, Gene's car had slid off the road near Salina (110 miles east of WaKeeney). The car had hit a culvert, as far as the highway patrolman could ascertain, and Gene had been killed instantly.

What was really difficult was that Mom had begged Gene to delay his trip back to school because of the bad weather. His answer was that he had to get back by Sunday afternoon as he had play practice. He was in a college production that was performing later that week. The consoling part of the accident was that no one else was involved. The highway patrolman had thoughtfully called the WaKeeney police chief, who found friends of my folks to deliver the devastating news rather than having them open the door to a police officer.

I'll never forget Dad sitting in the living room rocking chair for hours on end while his hair turned white. Mother never recovered completely from the shock either, but she continued to keep the family, including Dianne and me, moving forward.

At that time, we had no mortuary in town so Gene lay in an open casket in the office off the living room of our home until the funeral. The Presbyterian Church was overflowing for the service, including a number of Gene's friends from the University of Kansas.

During the summer, I canceled my registration to the University of Kansas and enrolled in The College of Emporia, a Presbyterian College in Emporia, Kansas.

Aside: *I have often wondered how my life would have been different had I attended KU.*

Out of the four family members who attended KU - my father, my brother, my sister and myself (I went to KU two summers for six week music camps - that counts), Dianne finally made it through. She graduated in 1961 with a Music Education Degree.

Resting In Peace

My Dad died on the farm November 15, 1982 at the age of 84. He went for a bike ride before lunch, had a meal with Mom, laid down on the living room couch for his normal afternoon nap and never woke up. My Mom passed away in Wamego, Kansas (where my sister lives) February 9, 1998 at the age of 94 after she developed complications from a fall.

Tornado Hits - June 1951

Just before midnight Tuesday, June 16, 1951, I was awakened by terrific winds rattling my bedroom windows with heavy rain lashing against the panes. At one point I thought the roof might blow away. After a while, the wind and the rain quit, and I went back to sleep. The following morning the phone rang, and I heard Mom talking with someone. When she hung up, she told us that a tornado had hit WaKeeney. Five people were killed and over 150 others were injured, 93 homes were destroyed and various other properties damaged in the county. The Red Cross came in to assist in the cleanup and many of us recent graduates helped with the aftermath.

A Tale of Survival

Later I heard that my "twin," Joyce, (a friend born at the same time, on the same day, in the same year as I was) had been awakened as she was flying through the air on her mattress being pummeled by the rain, hail and debris. She landed safely but was bruised and battered from the horrifying ordeal of the tornado. Her family's home was totally destroyed.

Bonus Sections

Don't miss the "bonus sections" where we have bloopers, old-timey jokes and cheers, autographs from my classmates and recipes from the homestead. What could be more fun than reading the bloopers as the iPad dictation tool did not necessarily hear what I actually spoke into the iPad. This is an up close and personal example of what technology can and cannot do.

Bloopers

Quirky Dictation Bloopers My Tribute To Technology!

I first begin writing my memoirs in 1974 on 3" x 5" and 4" x 6" notecards. Then "life" got in the way, and I did not get back to these notecards until the summer of 2006 when I retired from the life of a guest ranch co-owner/operator.

During that summer I typed all my notecards into a computer and printed the stories out on paper. Then "life" interrupted again, and not until 14 years later (due to 2020 COVID-19 stay at home orders) did I pick up my printed notes. During the ensuing 14 years the computer "froze" so corrections had to be made on the printed pages in longhand. On June 24, 2020, I began writing and rewriting my notes and memories in earnest and began using the "dictation to text function" on my iPad. The iPad had a hard time understanding my "Kansas" accent so there were many words and phrases that were lost in translation.

From my iPad the text went into the "cloud" where Dara, my fabulous copy editor, retrieved, deciphered and printed out the first draft via my office copier. After numerous hours of dictating, editing, correcting, and rewriting we decided that many of the "dictation bloopers" were so humorous and so entertaining they should be shared with you, the reader. It is hoped that you get as many laughs out of reading them as we did translating them.

Part I

My Dictation: I have led a Cinderella **life.**

What the iPad heard: I have led a Cinderella **lie.**

My Dictation: Mom reached under her bed and pulled out two **BB guns** – one for me and one for Gene. We were in heaven.

What the iPad heard: Mom reached under her bed and pulled out two **baby gir**ls – one for me and one for Gene. We were in heaven.

My Dictation: I did receive quite a few spankings as a child since I was not only an **ornery cuss** but also a really stubborn one.

What the iPad heard: I did receive quite a few spankings as a child since I was not only an **only cat** but a really stubborn one.

My Dictation: Living By Dad's **Tidbits** Of Wisdom

What the iPad heard: Living By Dad's **Tit Bits** Of Wisdom

My Dictation: Both Gene and I would try Mom's **patience** to the hilt.

What the iPad heard: Both Gene and I would try Mom's **patients** to the hilt.

My Dictation: I have two **scars.**

What the iPad heard: I have two **stars.**

My Dictation: There was a **barbed** wire fence on the side of the **barn.**

What the iPad heard: There was a **Bobbe** wire fence on the side of the **bar.**

My Dictation: I went yelling at the top of my **lungs.**

What the iPad heard: I went yelling at the top of my **longs.**

My Dictation: She pulled the skin together, threw on a disinfectant (probably **merthiolate** which we used for everything).

What the iPad heard: She pulled the skin together, threw on a disinfectant (probably **with a light** which we use for everything).

Skipping Between The Raindrops

My Dictation: **WaKeeney had a city** swimming pool.

What the iPad heard: **Joaquin, he had a shitty** swimming pool.

My Dictation:.. off we tumbled as the **cycle** careened on its side, out of control.

What the iPad heard: ...off we tumbled as the **psycho** careened on its side, out of control.

My Dictation: My speech impediment of not being able to pronounce my **R's** remained with me until my late 50s. **Upon** making collect phone calls...

What the iPad heard: My speech impediment, not being able to pronounce my **arse**, lasted me until my late 50s. **A bun** making collect phone calls...

 Part II

My Dictation: We enjoyed these care-free afternoons darting in and out of the **wheat** fields.

What the iPad heard: We enjoyed these care-free afternoons darting in and out of the **weak** fields

My Dictation: The second floor housed the principal's office, classrooms, a large music/meeting room and a **home economics** sewing room.

What the iPad heard: The second floor housed the principal's office, classrooms, a large music/meeting room and a **homemade** sewing room.

My Dictation: Since we had no cafeteria, all the **"townies"** trekked home for lunch.

What the iPad heard: Since we had no cafeteria, all the **Tonys** trekked home for lunch.

My Dictation: After all, if I **fought** everyone who made fun of my lack of height...

What the iPad heard: After all, if I **fart** everyone who made fun of my lack of height...

My Dictation: People tell me they **marvel** at my agility.

What the iPad heard: People tell me they **marble** at my agility.

My Dictation: My first day of school in first grade was very **traumatic** for me.

What the iPad heard: My first day of school in first grade was very **Trumatic** for me.

My Dictation: Why have I not been given a **middle name**?

What the iPad heard: Why have I not been given a **million name**?

My Dictation: I can see in my **mind's eye**.

What the iPad heard: I can see in my **mind Zai**.

My Dictation: He said that Walt Disney was **his uncle** and I believe it was true.

What the iPad heard: He said that Walt Disney was **a psycho** and I believe it was true.

My Dictation: They stayed a long time and **afterwards**.

What the iPad heard: They stayed a long time and **afterwords**.

My Dictation: ...then promptly **beat** them in a game.

What the iPad heard: ...then promptly **bitch** them in a game.

My Dictation: One captain tossed a **bat** to the other; wherever it was caught, the captains took turns placing hand over hand and the last one on top of the **bat** would get to choose the first player.

What the iPad heard: One captain tossed a **bad** to the other; wherever it was caught, the captains took turns placing hand over hand and the last one on top of the **bed** would get to choose the first player.

My Dictation: As you climb the hills the coming years,

May you travel in high and never **shift** gears,

What the iPad heard: As you climb the hills the coming years,

May you travel in high and never **shit** gears,

My Dictation: He was a gung-ho person with enthusiastic, different and **daring** ideas.

What the iPad heard: He was a gung-ho person with enthusiastic, different and **dairy** ideas.

My Dictation: Incidentally his real name was Jason **Ott.**

What the iPad heard: Incidentally his real name was Jason **Hot.** *(well, he was!)*

My Dictation: I was allowed to start taking lessons on the **cornet** in the fifth grade.

What the iPad heard: I was allowed to start taking lessons on the **corn head** in the fifth grade.

 Part III

My Dictation: We learned and could **sing** all the songs and dance all the jigs and **reels.**

What the iPad heard: We learned and could **seeing** all the songs and dance all the jigs and **reals.**

My Dictation: **Someday,** perhaps you and I will be able to jump!

What the iPad heard: **Sunday,** perhaps you and I will be able to jump!

My Dictation: ...teacher by the name of Bertie **Deines**.

What the iPad heard: teacher by the name of Bertie **dynasty**.

My Dictation: She also inspired them to **dream** great dreams.

What the iPad heard: She also inspired them to **green** great dreams.

My Dictation: ...remember giving him a few **wallops** and he quit his bullying **ways**.

What the iPad heard: ...remember giving him a few **wall ups** and he quit his bullying **Waze**.

My Dictation: as well as a very **sure** knowledge that I didn't like **any part of boxing**.

What the iPad heard: ...as well as a very **sheer** knowledge that I didn't like **the box**.

My Dictation: The **grade** school principal was a **law** to himself.

What the iPad heard: The **great** school principal was a **long** to himself.

My Dictation: Out of the clear blue **Mr. Noel** marched in the room.

What the iPad heard: Out of the clear blue **Mr. No well** marched in the room.

My Dictation: There was a group of us who **bummed** around together.

What the iPad heard: There was a group of us who **bumped** around together.

My Dictation: ...churches of various kinds, a Church of Christ, a Pentecostal church and an **Episcopalian** and several other denominations.

What the iPad heard: ...churches of various kinds, a Church of Christ, a Pentecostal church, and a **Pisca Palean** and several other denominations.

My Dictation: My "other biggie" was a lightweight **bed** jacket which **I conned** my grandmother into sewing.

What the iPad heard: My "other biggie" was a lightweight **bad** jacket which **icon** my grandmother into sewing.

My Dictation: The Home Economics classes were usually in a continual **uproar**... we would try to do anything to relieve the **dullness** in any way possible.

What the iPad heard: The Home Economics classes were usually in a continual **a poor**... we would try to do anything to relieve the **darkness** in any way possible.

My Dictation: The **staring** went on and on as the room got quieter.

What the iPad heard: The **steering** went on and on as the room got quieter

My Dictation: I still can't stand to **sew** and still can't **thread** a needle.

What the iPad heard: I still can't stand to **so** and still can't **read** a needle.

My Dictation: I went to work on a **kibbutz** in Israel.

What the iPad heard: I went to work on **the cabinets** in Israel.

My Dictation: We could **sit** up all night telling and **retelling** all the dumb, funny, stupid things we did over those years

What the iPad heard: We could **set** up all night telling and **retailing** all the dumb, funny, stupid things we did over those years

My Dictation: ...a moonlight bicycle ride out on our **unpaved, rutted** and lonely country road...

What the iPad heard: ...a moonlight bicycle ride out on our **unpaid, rotted** and lonely country road...

My Dictation: I gingerly **peeked out**; I was just about to bury my head **under the covers** when Peg broke out laughing.

What the iPad heard: I gingerly **picked out**; I was just about to bury my head **in the cupboard** when Peg broke out laughing.

My Dictation: Rain or shine we **hoofed** it to the cafeteria.

What the iPad heard: Rain or shine we **hooked** it to the cafeteria.

My Dictation: Tonight I have made a motto: "Share your **joys**."

What the iPad heard: Tonight I have made a motto: "Share your **Joyce**."

My Dictation: We went **careening** up to the field where the **Trego** County Free Fair was held.

What the iPad heard: We went **weaning** up to the field where the **Trigger** County Free Fair was held.

My Dictation: No sooner had the **pitcher** thrown the ball...

What the iPad heard: No sooner had a **picture** thrown the ball...

My Dictation: I'll never forget Gene's pride in me **when he** told my parents about the game.

What the iPad heard: I'll never forget Gene's pride in me **Winnie** told my parents about the game.

My Dictation: I **slipped** and my hand went crashing...

What the iPad heard: I **slept** and my hand went crashing...

My Dictation: ...at least one teacher was on **noon** duty, and the principal promptly **revved up** his little orange Volkswagen Beetle and away we dashed.

What the iPad heard: at least one teacher was on **new** duty, and the principal promptly **wrapped up** his little orange Volkswagen Beetle and away we dashed.

My Dictation: I'm still somewhat **ambidextrous**, as I had to write left-handed for several months. At commencement I received my diploma with my right hand **swathed** in a bandage.

What the iPad heard: I'm still somewhat **hampered extras**, as I had to write left-handed for several months. At commencement I received my diploma with my right hand **swabbed** in a bandage.

Part IV

My Dictation: My summers were spent on the tractor plowing with the **one-way discs**, driving the **wheat** truck.

What the iPad heard: My summers were spent on the tractor plowing with the **one-winging** discs, driving the **white** truck.

My Dictation: I had the bed of the 1937 Chevrolet **wheat truck** lined up with the **wheat chutes** on the combine.

What the iPad heard: I had the bed of the 1937 Chevrolet **weak truck** lined up with the **weed chutes** on the combine.

My Dictation: You had to watch the tractor driver as he would be **signaling** with his hand to speed up or to slow down.

What the iPad heard: You had to watch the tractor driver as he would be **singing** with his hand to speed up or to slow down.

My Dictation: I went to **Merne's** party.

What the iPad heard: I went to a **merge** party.

My Dictation: Her Dad **snored** louder than anyone I have ever heard. His **roars** blasted throughout the house.

What the iPad heard: Her Dad **snowed** louder than anyone I have ever heard. His **rowers** blasted throughout the house

My Dictation: We had several slumber **parties** upon the flat roof.

What the iPad heard: We had several slumber **parkings** upon the flat roof.

Skipping Between The Raindrops 213

My Dictation: The **bell** has **rung**! Let us **govern ourselves** accordingly.

What the iPad heard: The **belt** has **wrong**! Let us **governor sells** accordingly.

My Dictation: He could have put **Mel Tillis** to shame.

What the iPad heard: He could have put **mail tell us** to shame

My Dictation: He called **them in** and confronted **them** with his suspicions and they all fessed up.

What the iPad heard: He called **a man** in and confronted **him** with his suspicions and they all fessed up.

My Dictation: My friend took a terrific **ribbing** when her grade ended up as a D.

What the iPad heard: My friend took a terrific **ribbon** when her grade ended up as a D.

My Dictation: In my **yearbook** Mr. Johnston wrote:

What the iPad heard: In my **ear book** Mr. Johnston wrote:

My Dictation: Physical education was never one of the "choice" subjects in the **WaKeeney** school system.

What the iPad heard: Physical education was never one of the "choice" subjects in the **walk-in-the** school system.

My Dictation: We would run from one side of the house to the other, **bolting** the doors behind us.

What the iPad heard: We would run from one side of the house to the other, **building** the doors behind us.

My Dictation: One day a gang of us took off in the Hudson and went out to **Tidball's** ranch.

What the iPad heard: One day a gang of us took off in the Hudson and went out to **Ted balls** ranch.

My Dictation: We persuaded **Peg** to go into the **bar** at **Trego** Center to buy beer.

What the iPad heard: We persuaded **pig** to go into the **bat** at **Twinkle** Center to buy beer.

*My Dictation: I have never liked beer – **not Miller High Life** or any other kind.*

*What the iPad heard: I have never liked beer - **not military life** or any other kind.*

My Dictation: We went ice skating on one of the country **ponds**.

What the iPad heard: We went ice skating on one of the country **pines**.

My Dictation: Gene, Teg and many others lay down flat on the ice, starting at the **shoreline**... upon **hitting** dry land I was one frozen block of ice.

What the iPad heard: Gene, Teg and many others lay down flat on the ice, starting at the **soreline**... upon **hearing** dry land I was one frozen block of ice.

My Dictation: One of my classmates who was **present** at the incident...

What the iPad heard: One of my classmates who was **President** at the incident

My Dictation: The nicest hotel in downtown **Hays**, Kansas and was near the beginning of the parade **route**.

What the iPad heard: The nicest hotel in downtown **Haze**, Kansas and was near the beginning of the parade **root**.

My Dictation: To get the **operator**, you just turned the handle.

What the iPad heard: To get the **Opry**, you just turned the handle.

My Dictation: Guess what? I have the **mumps**. It sure made me sick!

What the iPad heard: Guess what? I have the **months**. It sure made me sick!

My Dictation: He was at the Kansas University **Relays** in Lawrence, KS.

What the iPad heard: He was at the Kansas University **Realize** in Lawrence, KS.

My Dictation: **Evelyn** was our senior class president and **all of** our class officers were women.

What the iPad heard: **Everyone** was our senior class president and **oliver** our class officers were women.

My Dictation: I was awakened by terrific winds rattling my bedroom windows and heavy rain lashing against the **panes**.

What the iPad heard: I was awakened by terrific winds rattling my bedroom windows and heavy rain lashing against the **pain**s.

And these were only a few! So much for technology!!!

Old-Timey Jokes And Cheers

There were so many references to the telling of jokes in my youth, my "book editor" challenged me to remember and re-tell some from 70 plus years ago. My memory banks could not retrieve any, but unbeknown to her I had saved file copies of high school newspapers *The Eye Opener* and *The Spotlight Review* where jokes were published on a weekly basis. *I knew if I held on to these long enough, they'd come in handy!*

Hope you enjoy the humor in the following little tidbits. *I wonder if they'll bring tears of laughter to our eyes as when they were first told to me in the <u>late-1940's</u>?*

An Irishman stopped before a grave in the cemetery containing a tombstone declaring: "Here lies a lawyer and an honest man."

He murmured to himself: "Who'd ever think that there be room for two men in one grave."

Mr. Elliott: You hammer nails like lightning, son.
Gene: You mean I'm really fast?
Mr. Elliott: No, you seldom strike in the same place.

A tramp knocked on the door of an old English inn named **George and the Dragon**. The landlady opened the door and the tramp asked, "Can you spare a poor man a bite to eat?" "No!" she shouted and slammed the door in his face.

After a few minutes, the tramp again knocked at the door and when the landlady appeared he said, "And now, could I have a few words with George?"

Peg: Do you suppose its bad luck to have a cat follow you?

Sharon: That all depends on whether you're a man or a mouse."

From Australia comes the story of the mama kangaroo who, after pausing several times one day to scratch her stomach, yanked two baby kangaroos from her pouch and thrashed them soundly for eating crackers in bed.

Pilot to tower, pilot to tower: Plane out of gas at 1,000 feet and 30 miles over ocean, what shall I do?

Tower to pilot, tower to pilot: Repeat after me: Our Father, who art in heaven...

Darlene: Why does a two legged stork stand on one leg?

Larry: Because if he lifted that one too, he would fall down.

Skipping Between The Raindrops

Jan: Why is it that whenever you were looking for something, you always find it in the last place you look?

Elaine: Because you stop looking when you find it.

Berniece: How can you prove that a horse has six legs?

Art: By saying he has fore legs in front, and two behind.

Howard: "If you don't marry me, I'll hurl myself over that 500 foot cliff!"

Charlotte: "Ha! That's a lot of bluff!"

Reformer: "And furthermore, hell is just filled with cocktails, roulette wheels, and naughty chorus girls."

Voice from the rear: "Oh, death, where is thy sting?"

Trego Community High School Cheers (TCHS)

Remember these...?

When you're up, you're up
When you're down, you're down
When you're up against Trego
You're upside down.

We are from Trego
And we couldn't be prouder
So if you can't hear us
We'll yell a little louder.
T - R - E - G – O! Tre-go!!

Hot potato, hot potato
Half-baked alligator
Ram Bam booilator
Chick Saw Daw
T-C-H-S
Rah Rah Rah!

The end.

Notes:

Autographs From My Classmates

Many of us kept Autograph Books in school, and it seems as if many of the kids could and did think of wild things to say. Where they came up with all the poetry, sayings, and off-key thoughts is beyond me. Here is a sampling of inscriptions from my Autograph Books; some signed and some not.

Dear double fault, I mean Judy
Remember 6-0, 6-0
Tough luck!!! – Larry

Footnote: If memory serves me correctly I think I challenged Larry to a winner take all tennis match when we were seniors. It was to have been a battle of the superiority of the sexes. By his comment, I believe it is obvious who came out on top – at least in this instance!

Dear Judy,
Gosh. How time flies. Just think only four years ago we were classified as green freshman. I have enjoyed having you as a classmate and friend (hope you get the five sets of twins you want!). Love, Hanora

Footnote: Hanora lived past us out in the country and sometimes we rode to school together.

    If you ever see a cat climb a tree
    Pull his tail and think of me.
    Charles, '52

Dear Judith
Ducks in the millpond
Fish in the ocean
Boys can't get married
'Til we girls take a notion.
        Janice

Part of the Gang!

Never ask of money spent,
Where the spender thinks it went,
Nobody was ever meant,
To remember or invent,
What he did with every cent.

Show this to your Mom when she asks you what you did with your allowance.
Kathleen, class of '52

Dear Judy,
I always liked being around you.
You are always full of jokes.
You are one of the best friends I have.
Your schoolmate,
          Anna

Dear Judy,
You asked me to write,
what shall it be?
Just two little words,
"Remember me"
          Cynthia

Dear Judy
A shotgun is a shotgun
A rifle is a rifle.
Look down the barrel
And you might get an eyeful.
As ever, Weedy
    Yours till Hungary fries
    Turkey in Greece.

Roses are red
Violets are blue
Salt is sour
And so are you.
          Malvin

Skipping Between The Raindrops

Dear Judy,
Now I lay me down to sleep
With the Ford parked on the street
If it should start before I awake,
I pray the Lord to put on the brakes.

And I love this one...
I love you little
I love you big
I love you like
A little pig.

Dear Judy
Roses are red
Violets are blue
Spring flowers are pretty
And so are you.
A pal, Carole Jean

Dear Judy,
When you get old and live by the river
Get a snail and save me the tail.
Everett

Boys think girls are lemons;
But that is just to tease!
Aren't the girls the lemons,
Boys like to squeeze?

Dear Judy,
While the golden sun is setting,
The earth no more you trod.
May your name be written
In the autograph of God.
Berniece

Roses are red,
Violets are blue,
I fell out of bed,
Dreaming of you

**Malcom, Curt and
'Ma' Judy**

Dear Judy,
 Remember when we chewed gum,
And rolled it into a ball,
To shoot at all the freshman,
In first hour study hall!
Shirley

I like to be naughty
I like to be nice
But just to be naughty
I'll sign my name twice.
Virginia
Virginia

I saw you in the ocean,
I saw you in the sea,
I saw you in the bathtub,
Oh, excuse me!
             Malcolm

Trees may whither
Flowers may die
Friends may forget you
But never will I
I'll always remember you as the best trumpet player in the band. - - - Carolyn

Dear Judy,
Oranges grow in California
Lemons grow there too
But it takes the state of Kansas
To grow a peach like you.
     Verna Lou

Love is like an onion
You taste it with delight
And once you get a mouthful
You wonder what made you bite!

> **Out behind the chicken house**
> **Down upon my knees**
> **Oh, it tickles me to death**
> **To hear the chicken sneeze.**

Roses are red and violets are blue
I have a bulldog Judy that looks just like you.

Brick is hard
And so is cement
My love for you
Is 100%

It tickles me so,
It makes me laugh
To think that you
Want my autograph.

When evening pulls the curtain
And pins it with a star
Remember you have a friend,
Although she may be far.

If you think you're in love
But still there is a question
Don't worry or fret
It may be indigestion.
      Dwayne

Shakespeare once said:
To thine own self be true
It must follow as the night the day
Doth canst not then be false to any man.

Skipping Between The Raindrops

Dear Judy,
It's really been swell knowing you and also going to all those parties and picnics together. Lots of luck in the future!!!
Apples in the spring time
Pictures in the fall
When it comes to nice girls
Judy beats them all.
Bert

Some people have a few friends,
　　Some people have a lot of friends,
But Judy is everybody's friend.
　　Footnote: How nice, wish I knew who wrote it.

In the parlor, there were three,
He, the parlor lamp, and she.
Three's a crowd, there's no doubt,
So the parlor lamp went out.

May your friends be added,
Your enemy subtracted,
Your joys multiplied,
And your sorrows divided.

Way down south where the cotton grows
An ant stepped on an elephant's toe.
Said the elephant with tears in his eyes
"Why don't you pick on someone your own size?"

I like you now,
Like you I will.
I like to look at you
Sitting on the window sill.

Dear Judy
I'm honored to be asked to write in your autograph book.
I'll always remember you as "outstanding" during your
high school years. I hope you will have fun at KU.
Also, don't forget the times we had in Latin II –
how we copied our lessons during class time!
And admirer and friend
Ronnie

Judith,
Wayback in this book
Where nobody will look
I'll sign my name
And close the book
Dean

Skipping Between The Raindrops

Recipes From The Homestead

These recipes and many more can be found in the delectable 267 page "Home Cooking" Harambe Oaks Ranch Recipe Cookbook.
(Order Form can be found on the last page of this recipe section.)

Notes:

Fruit Pie

My Mom's pies were SUPER!

Crust*		1 pie	2 pies	4 pies
Mix with fork	Crisco Butter Flavor Shortening	½ cup	1 cup	2 cups
	Flour	1½ cups	3 cups	6 cups
	Salt	½ tsp.	1 tsp.	2 tsp.
	Sugar	2 T	4 T	8 T
Add	Egg	1	2	4
Then add	Cold Water Enough so dough can roll			

Mix above and divide. Roll out dough to fit bottom and top of pie plate. Moisten crust edges with water to make crusts seal together. Or just put one crust on top.

* Or use pre-made pie crust mix. I like the Pillsbury brand.

Filling		1 pie	2 pies	4 pies
Mix	Apples, sliced**	4-6	8-10	16-20
	Sugar	1 cup	2 cups	4 cups
	Rounded Flour	2 T	4 T	½ cup
	Margarine	1-2 T	1-2 T	2-4 T
	Cinnamon, All-Spice	Dash	Dash	Dash
	Nutmeg, Cloves	Dash	Dash	Dash

** Or Peaches or 3 cups of Rhubarb (sliced)
Or use combination of apples, peaches, rhubarb, cherries!
Bake at 400 for 45-50 minutes.

Meatloaf With Topping

I have been adding 20-25% ground turkey. Tastes great!
Recipe from the kitchen of Hermena Rinker.

	Serves	6-8	16-20	35-40
Crumble	Bread	1 slice	2 slices	4 slices
Pour In	Milk	½ cup	1 cup	2 cups
Add & mix well	Ground Beef	1-1/2 lb.	3 lbs.	6 lbs.
	Eggs	1	2	4
	Chopped Onion	1 small	2 small	1 large
	Salt	Dash	¼ tsp.	½ tsp.
	Pepper	Dash	¼ tsp.	½ tsp.

Shape into one quart loaf pan. Bake approx. one hour at 350.

Last 10 minutes of baking time, drain grease from meatloaf and add topping.

Meatloaf Topping
This is wonderful!

	Serves	6-8	16-20	35-40
Mix	Brown Sugar	3 T	6 T	¾ cup
	Ketchup	¼ cup	½ cup	1 cup
	Nutmeg	¼ tsp.	½ tsp.	1 tsp.
	Mustard	1 tsp.	2 tsp.	4 tsp.

Sombrero Spread

What a great way to start an evening of playing Bridge!

From the kitchen of my sis, Dianne R. Childs

	Serves	6-8	12-15	25-30
Fry until brown	Hamburger	½ lb.	1 lb.	2 lbs.
	Onion, chopped	½ small	1 small	1 large
Add and Heat	Hot Catsup	¼ cup	½ cup	1 cup
	Chili Powder	1 ½ tsp.	1 T	2 T
	Salt	½ tsp.	1 tsp.	2 tsp.
Add	Red kidney beans, mashed	8 oz.	16 oz.	32 oz.
	Cheddar Cheese, shredded	½ cup	1 cup	2 cups
	Onion	½ small	1 small	1 large
	Stuffed Green Olives, sliced	¼ cup	½ cup	1 cup

Serve as hot dip with corn chips, crackers, or tostados.

Judy's Deelites

"One of my favorite cookie recipes - Easy and yummy!" Judy Rinker.

	Makes	1 pan	2 pans
Melt & pour into 9" x 13" pan.	Margarine or Butter	1 stick	2 sticks
Crumble into 9" x 13" pan	Assorted crumbs Any combination: graham crackers, Cookies, left-over anything	2 cups	4 cups
Sprinkle over crumbs	Chocolate bits, butterscotch bits, or white chocolate	1 cup +	2 cups +
More sprinkling	Coconut, any kind	1 cup	2 cups
	Pecans, chopped	1 cup	2 cups
	Add if desired: Craisins, M&Ms, any small candies	a few a few	a few a few
Drizzle over, **but do not ever stir anything!**	Eagle Brand Milk (Never stir, just fork a little if you must)	1 can	2 cans

Bake at 350 for 20-25 minutes.
Cut in pan to desired size squares. These freeze beautifully. Can be served hard or chewy – your choice.

Chocolate Beet Cake

Bet a million that no one will guess the "secret" ingredient – beets!
A truly fabulous cake, compliments of my Mom, Hermena Rinker.

	Makes	1 cake	2 cakes	4 cakes
Cream	Sugar	1½ cups	3 cups	6 cups
	Eggs	3	6	12
Mix	Salad Oil	1 cup	2 cups	4 cups
	Blended Drained Beets	1½ cups	3 cups	6 cups
Melt	German Sweet Chocolate (or 3 T baking chocolate With 1 T of oil)	2 Squares	4 squares	8 squares
	Beet Juice	3 T	6 T	12 T

Add above three mixtures together.

	Makes	1 cake	2 cakes	4 cakes
Add	Baking Soda	1 ½ tsp.	1 T	2 T
	Salt	½ tsp.	1 tsp.	2 tsp.
	Vanilla	1 tsp.	2 tsp.	4 tsp.
	Flour	1¾ cups	3½ cups	7 cups

Bake at 350 for 30 minutes in a 9" x 13" pan.
Any chocolate icing will top off this cake beautifully.
My basic icing is powered sugar, flavoring (almond or orange are wonderful), small amount of butter/oleo/margarine and water or milk.

Burnt Sugar Cake

Recipe from the kitchen of my favorite childhood neighbor Freda Spena

	Makes	1 cake	2 cakes
Burn to dark brown In Iron Skillet	Sugar	½ cup	1 cup
Add	Water	¼ cup	½ cup

Boil to syrup. Then cool slightly.

	Makes	1 cake	2 cakes
Cream	Butter	1 stick	2 sticks
	Sugar	2 tsp.	4 tsp.
	Egg Yolks	4	8
	Burnt Sugar Syrup*		

*Leave small amount of syrup in skillet for icing.

	Makes	1 cake	2 cakes
Sift	Flour	2 cups	4 cups
	Baking Powder	2 tsp.	4 tsp.
Add to Sugar alternately with flour	Milk	1 cup	2 cups
Whip	Egg whites	4	8
Fold in batter with egg whites	Vanilla	1 tsp.	2 tsp.

Pour in greased and floured 9"x 13" pan.
Bake at 350 for 35-40 minutes.

Icing

	Makes	1 cake	2 cakes
Mix in Skillet	Remaining Burnt Syrup		
	Milk or Cream	½ cup	1 cup
	Butter	1 T	2 T
Thicken with	Powdered Sugar	2 cups	4 cups
Chop	Nuts	½ cup	1 cup

Spread icing on cake. Garnish with chopped nuts, preferably pecans.

Rinker's Chili Soup

Fantastic flavors, nothing better for a hearty winter meal. From the kitchens of Hermena and Judy Rinker.

	Serves	10-12	20-24	40-50
Brown & Drain	Hamburger	1 lb.	2 lb.	4 lb.
Add	Worcestershire Sauce	2 tsp.	1 T+	2 T+
	Celery Salt, Onion Salt, Garlic Salt, Pepper & Salt	Dashes	Dashes	Dashes
	Chili Powder	1 T	2 T	4 T
	Chopped Onion, medium	1	2	4
	Chopped Green Pepper	1	2	4
	Chopped Celery	2 stalks	4 stalks	8 stalks

Cook 5 minutes.

	Serves	10-12	20-24	40-50
Add	Pork & Beans (or Pinto or Ranch Style)	16 oz.	32 oz.	64 oz.
	Tomatoes	28 oz.	56 oz.	112 oz.
	Tomato Juice	4 cups	8 cups	16 cups
	Beef Bouillon Cubes	4	8	16
	Water	4 cups	8 cups	16 cups

Bring to boil and cook 40-60 minutes. Great reheated next day or freeze for later.

Vegetable Beef Soup

Here's another robust dish for cool weather from the kitchens of Laverne Kellison, Hermena and Judy Rinker.

	Serves	10-12	20-24	40-50
Brown	Hamburger	1 lb.	2 lb.	4 lb.
Season with	Salt, Pepper, Garlic Salt Worcestershire Sauce	Dashes	Dashes	Dashes
Add	Onions	1	2	4
	Potatoes	2	4	8
	Carrots	2-4	4-8	10-12
	Celery	2 stalks	3-4 stalks	6-8 stalks
Then add	Chopped or shredded Cabbage	Handful	Handfuls	Handfuls
	Tomatoes (15 oz. can)	1 can	2 cans	4 cans
	Tomato Juice	4 cups	8 cups	16 cups
	Beef Bouillon Cubes	4	8	16
	Water	4 cups	8 cups	16 cups

Season to taste. Simmer until vegetables are done.

Crisp Oatmeal Cookies

Recipe from the kitchen of Hermena Rinker

	Makes	5 dozen	10 dozen
Combine & Beat thoroughly	Shortening	1 cup	2 cups
	White Sugar	¾ cup	1 ½ cups
	Brown Sugar	¾ cup	1 ½ cups
Add	Eggs	2	4
	Vanilla	1 tsp.	2 tsp.
	Water	3 T	6 T

Beat until light and fluffy.

	Makes	5 dozen	10 dozen
Sift	Flour	1 ½ cups	3 cups
	Salt	½ tsp.	1 tsp.
	Baking Soda	1 tsp.	2 tsp.
	Cinnamon	1 tsp.	2 tsp.

Add flour mix to sugar mix.

	Makes	5 dozen	10 dozen
Add	Uncooked Oatmeal	3 cups	6 cups
Optional To add	Pecans (preferred), or walnuts and/or Raisins	½ cup ½ cup	1 cup 1 cup

Scoop up 1 TB of dough and arrange on greased cookie sheet, two inches apart.
Bake at 350 for 10-12 minutes.
Remove cookie sheet & drop it on level stove top to slightly flatten warm cookies. This will create crinkle tops and taste delicious.

Order Forms

Use the order forms below for obtaining additional copies of the 267 page *"Home Cooking"* an Harambe Oaks Ranch Recipe Cookbook or for additional copies of *"Skipping Between The Raindrops"*.

ORDER FORM for *"Home Cooking"* cookbook

        Cut out, Fill in,   **JARinker**
          and Mail to: PO Box 108, Fischer, TX 78623

    Please mail _____ copies of the cookbook
       @ $20 each (includes shipping) to:

Name_____

Address_____

City, State, Zip_____

ORDER FORM for *Skipping Between The Raindrops, A Memoir*

        Cut out, Fill in,   **JARinker**
          and Mail to: PO Box 108, Fischer, TX 78623

Please mail _____ copies of Skipping Between The Raindrops
      @ $15 each (includes shipping) to:

Name_____

Address_____

City, State, Zip_____

    Or order more Memoirs online at: **Amazon.com**

Be On The Lookout For Book II And Book III Of This Fascinating Trilogy

Book I - Growing Up
  Skipping Between The Raindrops

Book II - Playing (world travels)

Book III - Working (teaching and guest ranch careers)

Coming Sooner or **Later**!!!

"I started Book I after supper and I did not stop reading until I finished it. I would say, it's a warm look into living in a small Kansas town in the 1930-1940's. I loved it!"
Janis H.

***To order copies of
Skipping Between The Raindrops
online go to: Amazon.com***

Why Not Share Your Story?

While working on this book, ***Skipping Between The Raindrops***, a few of us had lunch and/or dinner occasionally. At some point in our conversations, something that was said would remind us of an anecdote in the book, and we would be off and running in the telling of other stories we remembered from our youth.

So, why not try this yourself? Invite several family members, neighbors or friends in for coffee, lunch, Happy Hour, dinner, or a video/audio chat on the internet and sit around reliving memories from your childhoods.

You'll be amazed at how much everyone remembers and you will be pleasantly surprised about how many wonderful anecdotes come to mind. And it's so much fun sharing a laugh or two (or three or more) with your family, neighbors and friends.

To order copies of
Skipping Between The Raindrops
online go to: Amazon.com

Author Biography

Judy Rinker (JARinker) has been an educator, entertainer and organizer throughout her life. After graduating from high school, she earned several University Degrees, taught junior high school through college for 18 years, co-owned and operated a guest ranch for 27 years (chief cook and bottle washer) and has now been "free lancing" for the past 14 years.

She has never experienced a dull moment in her life which can be attributed to her ability to keep moving forward in her life's journey and to laugh at all of life's foibles. Judy considers life an ongoing adventure while exploring the four corners of the earth, making new friends everywhere and constantly striving to excel in all her endeavors.

Judy would like to give full credit for who she is to her family, her teachers and her friends who helped to furnish a firm foundation which has allowed her to continue *Skipping Between The Raindrops* throughout her life.

Made in the USA
Columbia, SC
23 November 2020